POEMS THAT EVERY CHILD SHOULD KNOW

THE LAND OF POESY

POEMS THAT EVERY CHILD SHOULD KNOW

A SELECTION OF THE BEST POEMS OF ALL TIMES FOR YOUNG PEOPLE

EDITED BY MARY E. BURT, 1850-1918, ELIZABETH

ed.

**ILLUSTRATED AND DECORATED
BY BLANCHE OSTERTAG**

Granger Index Reprint Series

BOOKS FOR LIBRARIES PRESS
PLAINVIEW, NEW YORK

PR
1175
.B8
1971

First Published 1904
Reprinted 1971

INTERNATIONAL STANDARD BOOK NUMBER
0-8369-6296-6

LIBRARY OF CONGRESS CATALOG CARD NUMBER
71-168776

PRINTED IN THE UNITED STATES OF AMERICA

PREFACE

Is THIS another collection of stupid poems that children cannot use? Will they look hopelessly through this volume for poems that suit them? Will they say despairingly, "This is too long," and "That is too hard," and "I don't like that because it is not interesting"?

Are there three or four pleasing poems and are all the rest put in to fill up the book? Nay, verily! The poems in this collection are those that children love. With the exception of seven, they are short enough for children to commit to memory without wearying themselves or losing interest in the poem. If one boy learns "The Overland Mail," or "The Recruit," or "Wynken, Blynken, and Nod," or "The Song in Camp," or "Old Ironsides," or "I Have a Little Shadow," or "The Tournament," or "The Duel," nine boys out of ten will be eager to follow him. I know, because I have tried it a dozen times. Every boy loves "Paul Revere's Ride" (alas! I have not been able to include it), and is ambitious to learn it, but only boys having a quick memory will persevere to the end. Shall the slower boy be deprived of the pleasure of reading the whole poem and getting its inspiring sentiment and learning as many stanzas as his mind will take? No, indeed. Half of such a poem is better than

none. Let the slow boy learn and recite as many
stanzas as he can and the boy of quick memory
follow him up with the rest. It does not help the
slow boy's memory to keep it down entirely or
deprive it of its smaller activity because he can-
not learn the whole. Some people will invariably
give the slow child a very short poem. It is often
better to divide a long poem among the children,
letting each child learn a part. The sustained
interest of a long poem is worth while. "The
Merman," "The Battle of Ivry," "Horatius at the
Bridge," "Krinken," "The Skeleton in Armour,"
"The Raven" and "Hervé Riel" may all profit-
ably be learned that way. Nevertheless, the child
enjoys most the poem that is just long enough, and
there is much to be said in favour of the selection
that is adapted, in length, to the average mind;
for the child hesitates in the presence of quantity
rather than in the presence of subtle thought. I
make claim for this collection that it is made up
of poems that the majority of children will learn
of their own free will. There are people who
believe that in the matter of learning poetry there
is no "*ought*," but this is a false belief. There is
a *duty*, even there; for every American citizen
ought to know the great national songs that keep
alive the spirit of patriotism. Children should
build for their future—and get, while they are
children, what only the fresh imagination of the
child can assimilate.

They should store up an untold wealth of heroic
sentiment; they should acquire the habit of
carrying a literary quality in their conversation;

Preface

they should carry a heart full of the fresh and delightful associations and memories connected with poetry hours to brighten mature years. They should develop their memories while they have memories to develop.

Will the boy who took every poetry hour for a whole school year to learn "Henry of Navarre" ever regret it, or will the children who listened to it? No. It was fresh every week and they brought fresh interest in listening. The boy will always love it because he used to love it. There were boys who scrambled for the right to recite "The Tournament," "The Charge of the Light Brigade," "The Star-Spangled Banner," and so on. The boy who was first to reach the front had the privilege. The triumph of getting the chance to recite added to the zest of it. Will they ever forget it?

I know Lowell's "The Finding of the Lyre." Attention, Sir Knights! See who can learn it first as I say it to you. But I find that I have forgotten a line of it, so you may open your books and teach it to me. Now, I can recite every word of it. How much of it can you repeat from memory? One boy can say it all. Nearly every child has learned the most of it. Now, it will be easy for you to learn it alone. And Memory, the Goddess Beautiful, will henceforth go with you to recall this happy hour.

MARY E. BURT.

The John A. Browning School, 1904.

CONTENTS

PART I

Contents

Contents

Contents

Contents

Contents

Contents

Contents

Contents

Contents

Contents

Contents

Contents

INDEX OF AUTHORS

Index of Authors

Index of Authors

PART I.

The Budding Moment

Poems That Every Child Should Know

The Arrow and the Song.

"The Arrow and the Song," by Longfellow (1807–82), is placed
first in this volume out of respect to a little girl of six years who used
to love to recite it to me. She knew many poems, but this was her
favourite.

I SHOT an arrow into the air,
It fell to earth, I knew not where;
For, so swiftly it flew, the sight
Could not follow it in its flight.

I breathed a song into the air,
It fell to earth, I knew not where;
For who has sight so keen and strong
That it can follow the flight of song?

Long, long afterward, in an oak
I found the arrow, still unbroke;
And the song, from beginning to end,
I found again in the heart of a friend.

HENRY W. LONGFELLOW.

The Babie.

I found "The Babie" in Stedman's "Anthology." It is placed in this volume by permission of the poet, Jeremiah Eames Rankin, of Cleveland (1828–), because it captured the heart of a ten-year-old boy whose fancy was greatly moved by the two beautiful lines:
> "Her face is like an angel's face,
> I'm glad she has no wings."

NAE shoon to hide her tiny taes,
  Nae stockin' on her feet;
Her supple ankles white as snaw,
  Or early blossoms sweet.

Her simple dress o' sprinkled pink,
  Her double, dimplit chin,
Her puckered lips, and baumy mou',
  With na ane tooth within.

Her een sae like her mither's een,
  Twa gentle, liquid things;
Her face is like an angel's face:
  We're glad she has nae wings.
                JEREMIAH EAMES RANKIN.

Let Dogs Delight to Bark and Bite.

"Let Dogs Delight to Bark and Bite," by Isaac Watts (1674–1748), and "Little Drops of Water," by Ebenezer Cobham Brewer (1810–97), are poems that the world cannot outgrow. Once in the mind, they fasten. They were not born to die.

LET dogs delight to bark and bite,
  For God hath made them so;
Let bears and lions growl and fight,
  For 'tis their nature to.

But, children, you should never let
　　Such angry passions rise;
Your little hands were never made
　　To tear each other's eyes.

ISAAC WATTS.

Little Things.

Little drops of water,
　　Little grains of sand,
Make the mighty ocean
　　And the pleasant land.

Thus the little minutes,
　　Humble though they be,
Make the mighty ages
　　Of eternity.

EBENEZER COBHAM BREWER.

He Prayeth Best.

These two stanzas, the very heart of that great poem, "The Ancient Mariner," by Samuel Taylor Coleridge (1772-1834), sum up the lesson of this masterpiece—"Insensibility is a crime."

FAREWELL, farewell! but this I tell
　　To thee, thou Wedding-Guest!
He prayeth well who loveth well
　　Both man and bird and beast.

He prayeth best who loveth best
　　All things, both great and small:
For the dear God who loveth us,
　　He made and loveth all.

SAMUEL T. COLERIDGE.

Twinkle, Twinkle, Little Star.

TWINKLE, twinkle, little star!
How I wonder what you are,
Up above the world so high,
Like a diamond in the sky.

When the glorious sun is set,
When the grass with dew is wet,
Then you show your little light,
Twinkle, twinkle all the night.

In the dark-blue sky you keep,
And often through my curtains peep,
For you never shut your eye,
Till the sun is in the sky.

As your bright and tiny spark
Guides the traveller in the dark,
Though I know not what you are,
Twinkle, twinkle, little star!

Pippa.

"Spring's at the Morn," from "Pippa Passes," by Robert Browning
(1812–89), has become a very popular stanza with little folks. "All's
right with the world" is a cheerful motto for the nursery and school-
room.

THE year's at the spring,
The day's at the morn;
Morning's at seven;
The hillside's dew pearled;

The lark's on the wing;
The snail's on the thorn;
God's in His heaven—
All's right with the world!

ROBERT BROWNING.

The Days of the Month.

"The Days of the Month" is a useful bit of doggerel that we need all through life. It is anonymous.

THIRTY days hath September,
April, June, and November;
February has twenty-eight alone.
All the rest have thirty-one,
Excepting leap-year—that's the time
When February's days are twenty-nine.

OLD SONG.

True Royalty.

"True Royalty" and "Playing Robinson Crusoe" are pleasing stanzas from "The Just So Stories" of Rudyard Kipling (1865–).

THERE was never a Queen like Balkis,
    From here to the wide world's end;
But Balkis talked to a butterfly
    As you would talk to a friend.

There was never a King like Solomon,
    Not since the world began;
But Solomon talked to a butterfly
    As a man would talk to a man.

She was Queen of Sabaea—
   And *he* was Asia's Lord—
But they both of 'em talked to butterflies
   When they took their walks abroad.

RUDYARD KIPLING.

(In "The Just So Stories.")

Playing Robinson Crusoe.

PUSSY can sit by the fire and sing,
   Pussy can climb a tree,
Or play with a silly old cork and string
   To 'muse herself, not me.
But I like Binkie, my dog, because
   He knows how to behave;
So, Binkie's the same as the First Friend was,
   And I am the Man in the Cave.

Pussy will play Man-Friday till
   It's time to wet her paw
And make her walk on the window-sill
   (For the footprint Crusoe saw);
Then she fluffles her tail and mews,
   And scratches and won't attend.
But Binkie will play whatever I choose,
   And he is my true First Friend.

Pussy will rub my knees with her head,
   Pretending she loves me hard;
But the very minute I go to my bed
   Pussy runs out in the yard,

And there she stays till the morning-light;
   So I know it is only pretend;
But Binkie, he snores at my feet all night,
   And he is my Firstest Friend!

RUDYARD KIPLING.

(In "The Just So Stories.")

My Shadow.

"My Shadow," by Robert Louis Stevenson" (1850-94), is one of
the most popular short poems extant. I have taught it to a great
many very young boys, and not one has ever tried to evade learning it.
Older pupils like it equally well.

I HAVE a little shadow that goes in and out with
   me,
And what can be the use of him is more than I
   can see.
He is very, very like me from the heels up to the
   head;
And I see him jump before me, when I jump into
   my bed.

The funniest thing about him is the way he likes
   to grow—
Not at all like proper children, which is always
   very slow;
For he sometimes shoots up taller like an india-
   rubber ball,
And he sometimes gets so little that there's none
   of him at all.

He hasn't got a notion of how children ought to
　　play,
'And can only make a fool of me in every sort of
　　way.
He stays so close beside me, he's a coward, you
　　can see;
I'd think shame to stick to nursie as that shadow
　　sticks to me!

One morning, very early, before the sun was up,
I rose and found the shining dew on every butter-
　　cup;
But my lazy little shadow, like an arrant sleepy-
　　head,
Had stayed at home behind me and was fast
　　asleep in bed.
　　　　　　　　　　　ROBERT LOUIS STEVENSON.

Little White Lily.

This poem (George Macdonald, 1828–) finds a place in this volume
because, as a child, I loved it. It completely filled my heart, and has
made every member of the lily family dear to me. George Macdonald's
charming book, "At the Back of the North Wind," also was my
wonder and delight.

LITTLE White Lily
Sat by a stone,
Drooping and waiting
Till the sun shone.

Little White Lily
Sunshine has fed;
Little White Lily
Is lifting her head.

Little White Lily
Said: "It is good
Little White Lily's
Clothing and food."
Little White Lily
Dressed like a bride!
Shining with whiteness,
And crownèd beside!

Little White Lily
Drooping with pain,
Waiting and waiting
For the wet rain.
Little White Lily
Holdeth her cup;
Rain is fast falling
And filling it up.

Little White Lily
Said: "Good again,
When I am thirsty
To have the nice rain.
Now I am stronger,
Now I am cool;
Heat cannot burn me,
My veins are so full."

Little White Lily
Smells very sweet;
On her head sunshine,
Rain at her feet.
Thanks to the sunshine,
Thanks to the rain,
Little White Lily
Is happy again.

GEORGE MACDONALD.

How the Leaves Came Down.

"How the Leaves Came Down," by Susan Coolidge (1845-), appeals to children because it helps to reconcile them to going to bed. "I go to bed by day" is one of the crosses of childhood.

"I'LL tell you how the leaves came down,"
    The great Tree to his children said:
"You're getting sleepy, Yellow and Brown,
    Yes, very sleepy, little Red.
    It is quite time to go to bed."

"Ah!" begged each silly, pouting leaf,
    "Let us a little longer stay;
Dear Father Tree, behold our grief!
    'Tis such a very pleasant day,
    We do not want to go away."

So, for just one more merry day
    To the great Tree the leaflets clung,
Frollicked and danced, and had their way,
    Upon the autumn breezes swung,
    Whispering all their sports among—

"Perhaps the great Tree will forget,
 And let us stay until the spring,
If we all beg, and coax, and fret."
 But the great Tree did no such thing;
 He smiled to hear their whispering.

"Come, children, all to bed," he cried;
 And ere the leaves could urge their prayer,
He shook his head, and far and wide,
 Fluttering and rustling everywhere,
 Down sped the leaflets through the air.

I saw them; on the ground they lay,
 Golden and red, a huddled swarm,
Waiting till one from far away,
 White bedclothes heaped upon her arm,
 Should come to wrap them safe and warm.

The great bare Tree looked down and smiled.
 "Good-night, dear little leaves," he said.
And from below each sleepy child
 Replied, "Good-night," and murmured,
 "It is *so* nice to go to bed!"

SUSAN COOLIDGE.

Willie Winkie.

"Wee Willie Winkie," by William Miller (1810-72), is included
in this volume out of respect to an eight-year-old child who chose it
from among hundreds. We had one poetry hour every week, and he
studied and recited it with unabated interest to the end of the year.

WEE WILLIE WINKLE rins through the town,
Up-stairs and doon-stairs, in his nicht-gown,
Tirlin' at the window, cryin' at the lock,
"Are the weans in their bed?—for it's now ten
 o'clock."

Hey, Willie Winkie! are ye comin' ben?
The cat's singin' gay thrums to the sleepin' hen,
The doug's speldered on the floor, and disna gie a
    cheep;
But here 's a waukrife laddie that winna fa' asleep.

Onything but sleep, ye rogue! glow'rin' like the
    moon,
Rattlin' in an airn jug wi' an airn spoon,
Rumblin' tumblin' roun' about, crowin' like a cock,
Skirlin' like a kenna-what—wauknin' sleepin' folk.

Hey, Willie Winkie! the wean's in a creel!
Waumblin' aff a body's knee like a vera eel,
Ruggin' at the cat's lug, and ravellin' a' her
    thrums,—
Hey, Willie Winkie!—See, there he comes!

Wearie is the mither that has a storie wean,
A wee stumpie stoussie that canna rin his lane,
That has a battle aye wi' sleep before he'll close
    an ee;
But a kiss frae aff his rosy lips gies strength anew
    to me.

WILLIAM MILLER.

The Owl and the Pussy-Cat.

"The Owl and the Pussy-Cat," by Edward Lear (1812–88), is placed here because I once found that a timid child was much strengthened and developed by learning it. It is a song that appeals to the imagination of children, and they like to sing it.

THE Owl and the Pussy-Cat went to sea
 In a beautiful pea-green boat;
They took some honey, and plenty of money
 Wrapped up in a five-pound note.
The Owl looked up to the moon above,
 And sang to a small guitar,
"O lovely Pussy! O Pussy, my love!
 What a beautiful Pussy you are,—
   You are,
 What a beautiful Pussy you are!"

Pussy said to the Owl, "You elegant fowl!
 How wonderful sweet you sing!
Oh, let us be married,—too long we have tarried,—
 But what shall we do for a ring?"
They sailed away for a year and a day
 To the land where the Bong-tree grows,
And there in a wood a piggy-wig stood
 With a ring in the end of his nose,—
   His nose,
 With a ring in the end of his nose.

"Dear Pig, are you willing to sell for one shilling
 Your ring?" Said the piggy, "I will."
So they took it away, and were married next day
 By the turkey who lives on the hill.

They dined upon mince and slices of quince,
    Which they ate with a runcible spoon,
And hand in hand on the edge of the sand
    They danced by the light of the moon,—
        The moon,
    They danced by the light of the moon.
                EDWARD LEAR.

Wynken, Blynken, and Nod.

"Wynken, Blynken, and Nod," by Eugene Field (1850–95), pleases
children, who are all by nature sailors and adventurers.

WYNKEN, Blynken, and Nod one night
    Sailed off in a wooden shoe,—
Sailed on a river of crystal light
    Into a sea of dew.
"Where are you going, and what do you wish?"
    The old moon asked the three.
"We have come to fish for the herring-fish
    That live in this beautiful sea;
    Nets of silver and gold have we,"
        Said Wynken,
        Blynken,
        And Nod.

The old moon laughed and sang a song,
    As they rocked in the wooden shoe;
And the wind that sped them all night long
    Ruffled the waves of dew;
The little stars were the herring-fish
    That lived in the beautiful sea.

"Now cast your nets wherever you wish,—
  Never afeard are we!"
So cried the stars to the fishermen three,
        Wynken,
        Blynken,
        And Nod.

All night long their nets they threw
  To the stars in the twinkling foam,—
Then down from the skies came the wooden shoe,
  Bringing the fishermen home:
'Twas all so pretty a sail, it seemed
  As if it could not be;
And some folk thought 'twas a dream they'd
      dreamed
  Of sailing that beautiful sea;
  But I shall name you the fishermen three:
        Wynken,
        Blynken,
        And Nod.

Wynken and Blynken are two little eyes,
  And Nod is a little head,
And the wooden shoe that sailed the skies
  Is a wee one's trundle-bed;
So shut your eyes while Mother sings
  Of wonderful sights that be,
And you shall see the beautiful things
  As you rock on the misty sea
  Where the old shoe rocked the fishermen three,—
        Wynken,
        Blynken,
        And Nod.

                          EUGENE FIELD.

The Duel.

"The Duel," by Eugene Field (1850–95), is almost the most popular humorous poem that has come under my notice. In making such a collection as this it is not easy to find poems at once delicate, witty, and graphic. I have taught "The Duel" hundreds of times, and children invariably love it.

THE gingham dog and the calico cat
Side by side on the table sat;
'Twas half-past twelve, and (what do you think!)
Nor one nor t'other had slept a wink!
The old Dutch clock and the Chinese plate
Appeared to know as sure as fate
There was going to be a terrible spat.
(*I wasn't there; I simply state*
What was told to me by the Chinese plate!)

The gingham dog went "bow-wow-wow!"
And the calico cat replied "mee-ow!"
The air was littered, an hour or so,
With bits of gingham and calico,
While the old Dutch clock in the chimney-place
Up with its hands before its face,
For it always dreaded a family row!
(*Now mind: I'm only telling you*
What the old Dutch clock declares is true!)

The Chinese plate looked very blue,
And wailed, "Oh, dear! what shall we do!"
But the gingham dog and the calico cat
Wallowed this way and tumbled that,
Employing every tooth and claw
In the awfullest way you ever saw—

And, oh! how the gingham and calico flew!
(*Don't fancy I exaggerate!*
I got my views from the Chinese plate!)

Next morning where the two had sat
They found no trace of the dog or cat;
And some folks think unto this day
That burglars stole the pair away!
But the truth about the cat and the pup
Is this: They ate each other up!
Now what do you really think of that!
(*The old Dutch clock it told me so,*
And that is how I came to know.)

EUGENE FIELD.

The Boy Who Never Told a Lie.

"The Boy Who Never Told a Lie" (anonymous), as well as "Whatever Brawls Disturb the Street," by Isaac Watts (1674-1748), are real gems. A few years ago they were more in favour than the poorer verse that has been put forward. But they are sure to be revived.

ONCE there was a little boy,
   With curly hair and pleasant eye—
A boy who always told the truth,
   And never, never told a lie.

And when he trotted off to school,
   The children all about would cry,
"There goes the curly-headed boy—
   The boy that never tells a lie."

And everybody loved him so,
   Because he always told the truth,
That every day, as he grew up,
   'Twas said, "There goes the honest youth."

And when the people that stood near
  Would turn to ask the reason why,
The answer would be always this:
  "Because he never tells a lie."

Love Between Brothers and Sisters.

WHATEVER brawls disturb the street,
  There should be peace at home:
Where sisters dwell and brothers meet,
  Quarrels should never come.

Birds in their little nests agree;
  And 'tis a shameful sight,
When children of one family
  Fall out and chide and fight.

                            ISAAC WATTS.

The Bluebell of Scotland.

OH where! and oh where! is your Highland laddie
    gone?
He's gone to fight the French for King George
    upon the throne;
And it's oh! in my heart how I wish him safe at
    home.

Oh where! and oh where! does your Highland
    laddie dwell?
He dwells in merry Scotland at the sign of the
    Bluebell;
And it's oh! in my heart that I love my laddie
    well.

If I Had But Two Little Wings.

"If I Had But Two Little Wings," by Samuel Taylor Coleridge (1772–1834), is recommended by a number of teachers and school-girls.

IF I had but two little wings
  And were a little feathery bird,
    To you I'd fly, my dear!
But thoughts like these are idle things
  And I stay here.

But in my sleep to you I fly:
  I'm always with you in my sleep!
    The world is all one's own.
And then one wakes, and where am I?
    All, all alone.

            SAMUEL T. COLERIDGE.

A Farewell.

"A Farewell," by Charles Kingsley (1819–75), makes it seem worth while to be good.

MY fairest child, I have no song to give you;
  No lark could pipe to skies so dull and gray;
Yet, ere we part, one lesson I can leave you
    For every day.

Be good, sweet maid, and let who will be clever;
  Do noble things, not dream them all day long:
And so make life, death, and that vast forever
    One grand, sweet song.

            CHARLES KINGSLEY.

Casabianca.

"Casabianca," by Felicia Hemans (1793–1835), is the portrait of a faithful heart, an example of unreasoning obedience. It is right that a child should obey even to the death the commands of a loving parent.

THE boy stood on the burning deck,
　　Whence all but him had fled;
The flame that lit the battle's wreck
　　Shone round him o'er the dead.

Yet beautiful and bright he stood,
　　As born to rule the storm;
A creature of heroic blood,
　　A proud though childlike form.

The flames rolled on—he would not go
　　Without his father's word;
That father, faint in death below,
　　His voice no longer heard.

He called aloud, "Say, father, say
　　If yet my task is done?"
He knew not that the chieftain lay
　　Unconscious of his son.

"Speak, father!" once again he cried,
　　"If I may yet be gone!"
And but the booming shots replied,
　　And fast the flames rolled on.

Upon his brow he felt their breath,
　　And in his waving hair;
And looked from that lone post of death,
　　In still, yet brave despair.

And shouted but once more aloud
  "My father! must I stay?"
While o'er him fast, through sail and shroud,
  The wreathing fires made way.

They wrapt the ship in splendour wild,
  They caught the flag on high,
And streamed above the gallant child
  Like banners in the sky.

Then came a burst of thunder sound—
  The boy—oh! where was he?
—Ask of the winds that far around
  With fragments strew the sea;

With mast, and helm, and pennon fair,
  That well had borne their part—
But the noblest thing that perished there
  Was that young, faithful heart.
                    FELICIA HEMANS.

The Captain's Daughter.

"The Captain's Daughter," by James T. Fields (1816–81), carries weight with every young audience. It is pointed to an end that children love—viz., trust in a higher power.

WE were crowded in the cabin,
    Not a soul would dare to sleep,—
It was midnight on the waters,
    And a storm was on the deep.

'Tis a fearful thing in winter
　　To be shattered by the blast,
And to hear the rattling trumpet
　　Thunder, "Cut away the mast!"

So we shuddered there in silence,—
　　For the stoutest held his breath,
While the hungry sea was roaring
　　And the breakers talked with Death.

As thus we sat in darkness,
　　Each one busy with his prayers,
"We are lost!" the captain shouted
　　As he staggered down the stairs.

But his little daughter whispered,
　　As she took his icy hand,
"Isn't God upon the ocean,
　　Just the same as on the land?"

Then we kissed the little maiden,
　　And we spoke in better cheer,
And we anchored safe in harbour
　　When the morn was shining clear.

JAMES T. FIELDS.

["The 'village smithy' stood in Brattle Street, Cambridge. There came a time when the chestnut-tree that shaded it was cut down, and then the children of the place put their pence together and had a chair made for the poet from its wood."

The Village Blacksmith.

Longfellow (1807–82) is truly the children's poet. His poems are as simple, pathetic, artistic, and philosophical as if they were intended to tell the plain every-day story of life to older people. "The Village Blacksmith" has been learned by thousands of children, and there is no criticism to be put upon it. The age of the child has nothing whatever to do with his learning it. Age does not grade children nor is poetry wholly to be so graded. "Time is the false reply."

UNDER a spreading chestnut-tree
    The village smithy stands;
The smith, a mighty man is he,
    With large and sinewy hands;
And the muscles of his brawny arms
    Are strong as iron bands.

His hair is crisp, and black, and long;
    His face is like the tan;
His brow is wet with honest sweat,
    He earns whate'er he can,
And looks the whole world in the face,
    For he owes not any man.

Week in, week out, from morn till night,
    You can hear his bellows blow;
You can hear him swing his heavy sledge,
    With measured beat and slow,
Like a sexton ringing the village bell,
    When the evening sun is low.

And children coming home from school
  Look in at the open door;
They love to see the flaming forge,
  And hear the bellows roar,
And catch the burning sparks that fly
  Like chaff from a threshing-floor.

He goes on Sunday to the church,
  And sits among his boys;
He hears the parson pray and preach,
  He hears his daughter's voice
Singing in the village choir,
  And it makes his heart rejoice.

It sounds to him like her mother's voice
  Singing in Paradise!
He needs must think of her once more,
  How in the grave she lies;
And with his hard, rough hand he wipes
  A tear out of his eyes.

Toiling,—rejoicing,—sorrowing,
  Onward through life he goes;
Each morning sees some task begin,
  Each evening sees it close;
Something attempted, something done,
  Has earned a night's repose.

Thanks, thanks to thee, my worthy friend,
  For the lesson thou hast taught!
Thus at the flaming forge of life
  Our fortunes must be wrought;
Thus on its sounding anvil shaped
  Each burning deed and thought.

                    HENRY W. LONGFELLOW.

Sweet and Low.

Sweet and low, sweet and low,
　Wind of the western sea,
Low, low, breathe and blow,
　Wind of the western sea!
Over the rolling waters go,
Come from the dropping moon and blow,
　Blow him again to me;
While my little one, while my pretty one
　sleeps.

Sleep and rest, sleep and rest,
　Father will come to thee soon;
Rest, rest, on mother's breast,
　Father will come to thee soon;
Father will come to his babe in the nest,
Silver sails all out of the west
　Under the silver moon:
Sleep, my little one, sleep, my pretty one,
　sleep.

Alfred Tennyson.

The Violet.

"The Violet," by Jane Taylor (1783–1824), is another of those dear old-fashioned poems, pure poetry and pure violet. It is included in this volume out of respect to my own love for it when I was a child.

Down in a green and shady bed
　A modest violet grew;
Its stalk was bent, it hung its head,
　As if to hide from view.

And yet it was a lovely flower,
   No colours bright and fair;
It might have graced a rosy bower,
   Instead of hiding there.

Yet there it was content to bloom,
   In modest tints arrayed;
And there diffused its sweet perfume,
   Within the silent shade.

Then let me to the valley go,
   This pretty flower to see;
That I may also learn to grow
   In sweet humility.

                JANE TAYLOR.

The Rainbow.

(A FRAGMENT.)

"The Rainbow," by William Wordsworth (1770–1850), accords with every child's feelings. It voices the spirit of all ages that would love to imagine it "a bridge to heaven."

MY heart leaps up when I behold
   A rainbow in the sky;
So was it when my life began,
So is it now I am a man,
So be it when I shall grow old,
   Or let me die!
The child is father of the man;
And I could wish my days to be
Bound each to each by natural piety.

        WILLIAM WORDSWORTH.

A Visit From St. Nicholas.

"A Visit From St. Nicholas," by Clement Clarke Moore (1779–1863), is the most popular Christmas poem ever written. It carries Santa Claus on from year to year and the spirit of Santa Claus.

'TWAS the night before Christmas, when all through
    the house
Not a creature was stirring, not even a mouse;
The stockings were hung by the chimney with care,
In hopes that St. Nicholas soon would be there;
The children were nestled all snug in their beds,
While visions of sugar-plums danced in their heads;
And mamma in her 'kerchief, and I in my cap,
Had just settled our brains for a long winter's nap,
When out on the lawn there arose such a clatter,
I sprang from the bed to see what was the matter.
Away to the window I flew like a flash,
Tore open the shutters and threw up the sash.
The moon on the breast of the new-fallen snow
Gave the luster of mid-day to objects below,
When, what to my wondering eyes should appear,
But a miniature sleigh, and eight tiny reindeer,
With a little old driver, so lively and quick,
I knew in a moment it must be St. Nick.
More rapid than eagles his coursers they came,
And he whistled, and shouted, and called them by
    name;
"Now, *Dasher!* now, *Dancer!* now, *Prancer* and
    Vixen !
On, *Comet !* on, *Cupid !* on, *Donder* and *Blitzen !*
To the top of the porch ! to the top of the wall !
Now dash away ! dash away ! dash away all !"

As dry leaves that before the wild hurricane fly,
When they meet with an obstacle, mount to the
sky;
So up to the house-top the coursers they flew,
With the sleigh full of toys, and St. Nicholas, too.
And then, in a twinkling, I heard on the roof
The prancing and pawing of each little hoof.
As I drew in my head, and was turning around,
Down the chimney St. Nicholas came with a bound.
He was dressed all in fur, from his head to his foot,
And his clothes were all tarnished with ashes and
soot;
A bundle of toys he had flung on his back,
And he looked like a peddler just opening his pack.
His eyes—how they twinkled! his dimples how
merry!
His cheeks were like roses, his nose like a cherry!
His droll little mouth was drawn up like a bow,
And the beard of his chin was as white as the
snow;
The stump of a pipe he held tight in his teeth,
And the smoke it encircled his head like a wreath;
He had a broad face and a little round belly,
That shook when he laughed, like a bowlful of
jelly.
He was chubby and plump, a right jolly old elf,
And I laughed when I saw him, in spite of myself;
A wink of his eye and a twist of his head,
Soon gave me to know I had nothing to dread;
He spoke not a word, but went straight to his
work,
And filled all the stockings; then turned with a
jerk,

And laying his finger aside of his nose,
And giving a nod, up the chimney he rose;
He sprang to his sleigh, to his team gave a whistle,
And away they all flew like the down on a thistle.
But I heard him exclaim, ere he drove out of sight
"*Happy Christmas to all, and to all a good-night.*"

CLEMENT CLARKE MOORE.

The Star-Spangled Banner.

O! SAY, can you see, by the dawn's early light,
  What so proudly we hailed at the twilight's last
    gleaming—
Whose broad stripes and bright stars, through the
      perilous fight,
  O'er the ramparts we watched were so gallantly
    streaming!
And the rocket's red glare, the bombs bursting in
    air,
Gave proof through the night that our flag was
    still there;
O! say, does that star-spangled banner yet wave
O'er the land of the free, and the home of the brave?

On that shore dimly seen through the mists of the
    deep,
  Where the foe's haughty host in dread silence
    reposes,
What is that which the breeze, o'er the towering
    steep,
  As it fitfully blows, now conceals, now discloses?

Now it catches the gleam of the morning's first
beam,
In full glory reflected now shines on the stream;
'Tis the star-spangled banner; O long may it wave
O'er the land of the free, and the home of the brave !

And where is that band who so vauntingly swore
That the havoc of war and the battle's confusion
A home and a country should leave us no more?
Their blood has washed out their foul footsteps'
pollution.
No refuge could save the hireling and slave
From the terror of flight, or the gloom of the grave;
And the star-spangled banner in triumph doth
wave
O'er the land of the free, and the home of the brave.

O ! thus be it ever, when freemen shall stand
Between their loved homes and the war's
desolation !
Blest with victory and peace, may the heav'n-
rescued land
Praise the power that hath made and preserved
us a nation.
Then conquer we must, for our cause it is just,
And this be our motto—"*In God is our trust*":
And the star-spangled banner in triumph shall
wave
O'er the land of the free, and the home of the brave.

Father William.

"Father William," a parody by Lewis Carroll (1833-), is even
more clever than the original. Harmless fun brightens the world.
It takes a real genius to create wit that carries no sting.

"You are old, Father William," the young man said,
　"And your hair has become very white;
And yet you incessantly stand on your head—
　Do you think, at your age, it is right?"

"In my youth," Father William replied to his son,
　"I feared it might injure the brain;
But now that I'm perfectly sure I have none,
　Why, I do it again and again."

"You are old," said the youth, "as I mentioned
　　before,
　And have grown most uncommonly fat;
Yet you turned a back-somersault in at the door—
　Pray, what is the reason of that?"

"In my youth," said the sage, as he shook his
　　gray locks,
　"I kept all my limbs very supple
By the use of this ointment—one shilling the box—
　Allow me to sell you a couple."

"You are old," said the youth, "and your jaws
　　are too weak
　For anything tougher than suet;
Yet you finished the goose, with the bones and
　　the beak:
　Pray, how did you manage to do it?"

"In my youth," said his father, "I took to the
    law,
  And argued each case with my wife;
And the muscular strength which it gave to my
    jaw
  Has lasted the rest of my life."

"You are old," said the youth; "one would hardly
    suppose
  That your eye was as steady as ever;
Yet you balanced an eel on the end of your nose—
  What made you so awfully clever?"

"I have answered three questions, and that is
    enough,"
  Said his father, "don't give yourself airs!
Do you think I can listen all day to such stuff?
  Be off, or I'll kick you down-stairs!"

                                LEWIS CARROLL.

  ("Alice in Wonderland.")

The Nightingale and the Glow-worm.

"The Nightingale," by William Cowper (1731–1800), is a favourite
with a teacher of good taste, and I include it at her request.

  A NIGHTINGALE, that all day long
  Had cheered the village with his song,
  Nor yet at eve his note suspended,
  Nor yet when eventide was ended,
  Began to feel, as well he might,
  The keen demands of appetite;
  When, looking eagerly around,
  He spied far off, upon the ground,

A something shining in the dark,
And knew the glow-worm by his spark;
So, stooping down from hawthorn top,
He thought to put him in his crop.
The worm, aware of his intent,
Harangued him thus, right eloquent:
"Did you admire my lamp," quoth he,
"As much as I your minstrelsy,
You would abhor to do me wrong,
As much as I to spoil your song;
For 'twas the self-same power divine,
Taught you to sing and me to shine;
That you with music, I with light,
Might beautify and cheer the night."
The songster heard his short oration,
And warbling out his approbation,
Released him, as my story tells,
And found a supper somewhere else.

WILLIAM COWPER.

PART II.

The Little Child

PART II

The Frost.

"Jack Frost," by Hannah Flagg Gould (1789–1865), is perhaps a hundred years old, but he is the same rollicking fellow to-day as of yore. The poem puts his merry pranks to the front and prepares the way for science to give him a true analysis.

THE Frost looked forth, one still, clear night,
And whispered, "Now I shall be out of sight;
So through the valley and over the height,
    In silence I'll take my way:
I will not go on with that blustering train,
The wind and the snow, the hail and the rain,
Who make so much bustle and noise in vain,
    But I'll be as busy as they."

Then he flew to the mountain and powdered its
        crest;
He lit on the trees, and their boughs he dressed
In diamond beads—and over the breast
    Of the quivering lake he spread
A coat of mail, that it need not fear
The downward point of many a spear
That hung on its margin far and near,
    Where a rock could rear its head.

He went to the windows of those who slept,
And over each pane, like a fairy, crept;
Wherever he breathed, wherever he slept,
    By the light of the moon were seen

Most beautiful things—there were flowers and trees;
There were bevies of birds and swarms of bees;
There were cities with temples and towers, and
    these
  All pictured in silver sheen !

But he did one thing that was hardly fair;
He peeped in the cupboard, and finding there
That all had forgotten for him to prepare—
  "Now just to set them a-thinking,
I'll bite this basket of fruit," said he,
"This costly pitcher I'll burst in three,
And the glass of water they've left for me
  Shall '*tchich !*' to tell them I'm drinking."
                          HANNAH FLAGG GOULD.

The Owl.

WHEN cats run home and light is come,
  And dew is cold upon the ground,
And the far-off stream is dumb,
  And the whirring sail goes round,
  And the whirring sail goes round;
    Alone and warming his five wits,
    The white owl in the belfry sits.

When merry milkmaids click the latch,
  And rarely smells the new-mown hay,
And the cock hath sung beneath the thatch
  Twice or thrice his roundelay,
  Twice or thrice his roundelay;
    Alone and warming his five wits,
    The white owl in the belfry sits.
                          ALFRED TENNYSON.

Little Billee.

"Little Billee," by William Makepeace Thackeray (1811–63), finds a place here because it carries a good lesson good-naturedly rendered. An accomplished teacher recommends it, and I recollect two young children in Chicago who sang it frequently for years without getting tired of it.

THERE were three sailors of Bristol city
  Who took a boat and went to sea.
But first with beef and captain's biscuits
  And pickled pork they loaded she.

There was gorging Jack and guzzling Jimmy,
  And the youngest he was little Billee.
Now when they got so far as the Equator
  They'd nothing left but one split pea.

Says gorging Jack to guzzling Jimmy,
  "I am extremely hungaree."
To gorging Jack says guzzling Jimmy,
  "We've nothing left, us must eat we."

Says gorging Jack to guzzling Jimmy,
  "With one another, we shouldn't agree!
There's little Bill, he's young and tender,
  We're old and tough, so let's eat he."

"Oh! Billy, we're going to kill and eat you,
  So undo the button of your chemie."
When Bill received this information
  He used his pocket-handkerchie.

"First let me say my catechism,
  Which my poor mammy taught to me."
"Make haste, make haste," says guzzling Jimmy
  While Jack pulled out his snickersnee.

So Billy went up to the main-topgallant mast,
   And down he fell on his bended knee.
He scarce had come to the Twelfth Commandment
   When up he jumps, "There's land I see.

"Jerusalem and Madagascar,
   And North and South Amerikee:
There's the British flag a-riding at anchor,
   With Admiral Napier, K. C. B."

So when they got aboard of the Admiral's
   He hanged fat Jack and flogged Jimmee;
But as for little Bill, he made him
   The Captain of a Seventy-three.
             WILLIAM MAKEPEACE THACKERAY.

The Butterfly and the Bee.

"The Butterfly and the Bee," by William Lisle Bowles (1762–1850),
is recommended by some school-girls. It carries a lesson in favour
of the worker.

METHOUGHT I heard a butterfly
   Say to a labouring bee:
"Thou hast no colours of the sky
   On painted wings like me."

"Poor child of vanity! those dyes,
   And colours bright and rare,"
With mild reproof, the bee replies,
   "Are all beneath my care.

"Content I toil from morn to eve,
   And scorning idleness,
To tribes of gaudy sloth I leave
   The vanity of dress."
             WILLIAM LISLE BOWLES.

An Incident of the French Camp.

"An Incident of the French Camp," by Robert Browning (1812–89), is included in this volume out of regard to a boy of eight years who did not care for many poems, but this one stirred his heart to its depths.

You know, we French storm'd Ratisbon:
    A mile or so away
On a little mound, Napoleon
    Stood on our storming-day;
With neck out-thrust, you fancy how,
    Legs wide, arms lock'd behind,
As if to balance the prone brow
    Oppressive with its mind.

Just as perhaps he mus'd "My plans
    That soar, to earth may fall,
Let once my army leader Lannes
    Waver at yonder wall,"—
Out 'twixt the battery smokes there flew
    A rider, bound on bound
Full-galloping; nor bridle drew
    Until he reach'd the mound.

Then off there flung in smiling joy,
    And held himself erect
By just his horse's mane, a boy:
    You hardly could suspect—
(So tight he kept his lips compress'd,
    Scarce any blood came through)
You look'd twice ere you saw his breast
    Was all but shot in two.

"Well," cried he, "Emperor, by God's grace
   We've got you Ratisbon!
The Marshal's in the market-place,
   And you'll be there anon
To see your flag-bird flap his vans
   Where I, to heart's desire,
Perched him!" The chief's eye flashed; his
    plans
   Soared up again like fire.

The chief's eye flashed; but presently
   Softened itself, as sheathes
A film the mother-eagle's eye
   When her bruised eaglet breathes;
"You're wounded!" "Nay," the soldier's
   pride
   Touched to the quick, he said:
"I'm killed, Sire!" And his chief beside,
   Smiling the boy fell dead.

ROBERT BROWNING.

Robert of Lincoln.

"Robert of Lincoln," by William Cullen Bryant (1794–1878), is one of the finest bird poems ever written. It finds a place here because I have seen it used effectively as a memory gem in the Cook County Normal School (Colonel Parker's school), year after year, and because my own pupils invariably like to commit it to memory. With the child of six to the student of twenty years it stands a source of delight.

MERRILY swinging on brier and weed,
   Near to the nest of his little dame,
Over the mountain-side or mead,
   Robert of Lincoln is telling his name.
      Bob-o'-link, bob-o'-link,
      Spink, spank, spink,

Snug and safe is this nest of ours,
Hidden among the summer flowers.
　　　Chee, chee, chee.

Robert of Lincoln is gayly dressed,
　　Wearing a bright, black wedding-coat;
White are his shoulders, and white his crest,
　　Hear him call in his merry note,
　　　　Bob-o'-link, bob-o'-link,
　　　　Spink, spank, spink,
Look what a nice, new coat is mine;
Sure there was never a bird so fine.
　　　Chee, chee, chee.

Robert of Lincoln's Quaker wife,
　　Pretty and quiet, with plain brown wings,
Passing at home a patient life,
　　Broods in the grass while her husband sings,
　　　　Bob-o'-link, bob-o'-link,
　　　　Spink, spank, spink,
Brood, kind creature, you need not fear
Thieves and robbers while I am here.
　　　Chee, chee, chee.

Modest and shy as a nun is she;
　　One weak chirp is her only note;
Braggart, and prince of braggarts is he,
　　Pouring boasts from his little throat,
　　　　Bob-o'-link, bob-o'-link,
　　　　Spink, spank, spink,
Never was I afraid of man,
Catch me, cowardly knaves, if you can.
　　　Chee, chee, chee.

Six white eggs on a bed of hay,
  Flecked with purple, a pretty sight:
There as the mother sits all day,
  Robert is singing with all his might,
    Bob-o'-link, bob-o'-link,
    Spink, spank, spink,
Nice good wife that never goes out,
Keeping house while I frolic about.
    Chee, chee, chee.

Soon as the little ones chip the shell,
  Six wide mouths are open for food;
Robert of Lincoln bestirs him well,
  Gathering seeds for the hungry brood:
    Bob-o'-link, bob-o'-iink,
    Spink, spank, spink,
This new life is likely to be
Hard for a gay young fellow like me.
    Chee, chee, chee.

Robert of Lincoln at length is made
  Sober with work, and silent with care,
Off is his holiday garment laid,
  Half forgotten that merry air,
    Bob-o'-link, bob-o'-link,
    Spink; spank, spink,
Nobody knows but my mate and I,
Where our nest and our nestlings lie.
    Chee, chee, chee.

Summer wanes; the children are grown;
  Fun and frolic no more he knows,

Robert of Lincoln's a hum-drum drone;
  Off he flies, and we sing as he goes,
    Bob-o'-link, bob-o'-link,
    Spink, spank, spink,
When you can pipe that merry old strain,
Robert of Lincoln, come back again.
    Chee, chee, chee.
                          WILLIAM CULLEN BRYANT.

Old Grimes.

"Old Grimes" is an heirloom, an antique gem. We learn it as a matter of course for its sparkle and glow.

OLD Grimes is dead; that good old man,
  We ne'er shall see him more;
He used to wear a long, black coat,
  All buttoned down before.

His heart was open as the day,
  His feelings all were true;
His hair was some inclined to gray,
  He wore it in a queue.

He lived at peace with all mankind,
  In friendship he was true;
His coat had pocket-holes behind,
  His pantaloons were blue.

He modest merit sought to find,
  And pay it its desert;
He had no malice in his mind,
  No ruffles on his shirt.

His neighbours he did not abuse,
  Was sociable and gay;
He wore large buckles on his shoes,
  And changed them every day.

His knowledge, hid from public gaze,
  He did not bring to view,
Nor make a noise town-meeting days,
  As many people do.

His worldly goods he never threw
  In trust to fortune's chances,
But lived (as all his brothers do)
  In easy circumstances.

Thus undisturbed by anxious cares
  His peaceful moments ran;
And everybody said he was
  A fine old gentleman.

                    ALBERT GORTON GREENE.

Song of Life.

A TRAVELLER on a dusty road
  Strewed acorns on the lea;
And one took root and sprouted up,
  And grew into a tree.
Love sought its shade at evening-time,
  To breathe its early vows;
And Age was pleased, in heights of noon,
  To bask beneath its boughs.

The dormouse loved its dangling twigs,
  The birds sweet music bore—
It stood a glory in its place,
  A blessing evermore.

A little spring had lost its way
  Amid the grass and fern;
A passing stranger scooped a well
  Where weary men might turn.
He walled it in, and hung with care
  A ladle on the brink;
He thought not of the deed he did,
  But judged that Toil might drink.
He passed again; and lo! the well,
  By summer never dried,
Had cooled ten thousand parchéd tongues,
  And saved a life beside.

A nameless man, amid the crowd
  That thronged the daily mart,
Let fall a word of hope and love,
  Unstudied from the heart,
A whisper on the tumult thrown,
  A transitory breath,
It raised a brother from the dust,
  It saved a soul from death.
O germ! O fount! O word of love!
  O thought at random cast!
Ye were but little at the first,
  But mighty at the last.

                                CHARLES MACKAY.

Fairy Song.

SHED no tear!   O shed no tear!
The flower will bloom another year.
Weep no more!   O, weep no more!
Young buds sleep in the root's white core.
Dry your eyes!   Oh! dry your eyes!
For I was taught in Paradise
To ease my breast of melodies—
            Shed no tear.

Overhead! look overhead!
'Mong the blossoms white and red—
Look up, look up.   I flutter now
On this flush pomegranate bough.
See me! 'tis this silvery bell
Ever cures the good man's ill.
Shed no tear!   O, shed no tear!
The flowers will bloom another year.
Adieu, adieu—I fly, adieu,
I vanish in the heaven's blue—
            Adieu, adieu!

                            JOHN KEATS.

A Boy's Song.

"A Boy's Song," by James Hogg (1770-1835), is a sparkling poem, very attractive to children.

WHERE the pools are bright and deep,
Where the gray trout lies asleep,
Up the river and o'er the lea,
That's the way for Billy and me.

Where the blackbird sings the latest,
Where the hawthorn blooms the sweetest,
Where the nestlings chirp and flee,
That's the way for Billy and me.

Where the mowers mow the cleanest,
Where the hay lies thick and greenest,
There to trace the homeward bee,
That's the way for Billy and me.

Where the hazel bank is steepest,
Where the shadow falls the deepest,
Where the clustering nuts fall free,
That's the way for Billy and me.

Why the boys should drive away
Little sweet maidens from the play,
Or love to banter and fight so well,
That's the thing I never could tell.

But this I know, I love to play,
Through the meadow, among the hay;
Up the water and o'er the lea,
That's the way for Billy and me.

JAMES HOGG.

Buttercups and Daisies.

BUTTERCUPS and daisies,
　　Oh, the pretty flowers;
Coming ere the spring time,
　　To tell of sunny hours.

While the trees are leafless,
  While the fields are bare,
Buttercups and daisies
  Spring up here and there.

Ere the snowdrop peepeth,
  Ere the crocus bold,
Ere the early primrose
  Opes its paly gold,
Somewhere on the sunny bank
  Buttercups are bright;
Somewhere 'mong the frozen grass
  Peeps the daisy white.

Little hardy flowers,
  Like to children poor,
Playing in their sturdy health
  By their mother's door,
Purple with the north wind,
  Yet alert and bold;
Fearing not, and caring not,
  Though they be a-cold!

What to them is winter!
  What are stormy showers!
Buttercups and daisies
  Are these human flowers!
He who gave them hardships
  And a life of care,
Gave them likewise hardy strength
  And patient hearts to bear.

MARY HOWITT.

The Rainbow.

TRIUMPHAL arch, that fills the sky
　　When storms prepare to part,
I ask not proud Philosophy
　　To teach me what thou art.

Still seem, as to my childhood's sight,
　　A midway station given,
For happy spirits to alight,
　　Betwixt the earth and heaven.

　　　　　　　THOMAS CAMPBELL.

Old Ironsides.

"Old Ironsides," by Oliver Wendell Holmes (1809-94), is learned readily. Children are untouched by the commercial spirit which is the reproach of this age. "Ingratitude is the vice of republics," and this poem puts to shame the love of money and the spirit of ingratitude that could let a national servant become a wreck.

AY, tear her tattered ensign down!
　　Long has it waved on high,
And many an eye has danced to see
　　That banner in the sky;
Beneath it rung the battle shout,
　　And burst the cannon's roar;—
The meteor of the ocean air
　　Shall sweep the clouds no more.

Her deck, once red with heroes' blood,
　　Where knelt the vanquished foe,
When winds were hurrying o'er the flood,
　　And waves were white below,

No more shall feel the victor's tread,
  Or know the conquered knee;
The harpies of the shore shall pluck
  The eagle of the sea!

O, better that her shattered hulk
  Should sink beneath the wave;
Her thunders shook the mighty deep,
  And there should be her grave;
Nail to the mast her holy flag,
  Set every threadbare sail,
And give her to the god of storms,
  The lightning and the gale!

OLIVER WENDELL HOLMES.

Little Orphant Annie.

"Little Orphant Annie" certainly earns her "board and keep" when she has "washed the dishes," "swept up the crumbs," "driven the chickens from the porch," and done all the other odds and ends of work on a farm. The poet, James Whitcomb Riley (1853-), has shown how truly a little child may be overtaxed and yet preserve a brave spirit and keen imagination. Children invariably love to learn this poem.

LITTLE Orphant Annie's come to our house to stay,
An' wash the cups and saucers up, an' brush the
  crumbs away,
An' shoo the chickens off the porch, an' dust the
  hearth, an' sweep,
An' make the fire, an' bake the bread, an' earn her
  board-an'-keep;
An' all us other children, when the supper things
  is done,
We set around the kitchen fire an' has the mostest
  fun

A-list'nin' to the witch-tales 'at Annie tells about,
An' the Gobble-uns 'at gits you
     Ef you
       Don't
         Watch
           Out!

Onc't they was a little boy wouldn't say his
    pray'rs—
An' when he went to bed at night, away up-stairs,
His mammy heerd him holler, an' his daddy heerd
    him bawl,
An' when they turn't the kivvers down, he wasn't
    there at all!
An' they seeked him in the rafter-room, an' cubby-
    hole, an' press,
An' seeked him up the chimbly flue, an' ever'-
    wheres, I guess;
But all they ever found was thist his pants an'
    roundabout!
An' the Gobble-uns'll git you
       Ef you
        Don't
         Watch
          Out!

An' one time a little girl 'ud allus laugh an' grin,
An' make fun of ever' one, an' all her blood-an'-kin;
An' onc't when they was "company," an' ole folks
    was there,
She mocked 'em an' shocked 'em, an' said she
    didn't care!

An' thist as she kicked her heels, an' turn't to run
  an' hide,
They was two great big Black Things a-standin'
  by her side,
An' they snatched her through the ceilin' 'fore
  she knowed what she's about !
An' the Gobble-uns'll git you
              Ef you
                Don't
                  Watch
                    Out !

An' little Orphant Annie says, when the blaze is
  blue,
An' the lampwick sputters, an' the wind goes
  woo-oo !
An' you hear the crickets quit, an' the moon is
  gray,
An' the lightnin'-bugs in dew is all squenched
  away,—
You better mind yer parents, an' yer teachers
  fond an' dear,
An' churish them 'at loves you, an' dry the or-
  phant's tear,
An' he'p the pore an' needy ones 'at clusters all
  about,
Er the Gobble-uns'll git you
              Ef you
                Don't
                  Watch
                    Out !
                  JAMES WHITCOMB RILEY.

O Captain! My Captain!

"O Captain! My Captain!" by Walt Whitman (1819–92), is placed here out of compliment to a little boy aged ten who wanted to recite it once a week for a year. This song and Edwin Markham's poem on Lincoln are two of the greatest tributes ever paid to that hero

O CAPTAIN! my Captain! our fearful trip is done,
The ship has weathered every rack, the prize we
    sought is won,
The port is near, the bells I hear, the people all
    exulting,
While follow eyes the steady keel, the vessel grim
    and daring;
    But O heart! heart! heart!
        O the bleeding drops of red,
            Where on the deck my Captain lies,
                Fallen cold and dead.

O Captain! my Captain! rise up and hear the bells;
Rise up—for you the flag is flung—for you the
    bugle trills,
For you bouquets and ribboned wreaths—for you
    the shores a-crowding,
For you they call, the swaying mass, their eager
    faces turning;
    Here Captain! dear father!
        This arm beneath your head!
            It is some dream that on the deck
                You've fallen cold and dead.

My Captain does not answer, his lips are pale and
    still,
My father does not feel my arm, he has no pulse
    nor will,

The ship is anchored safe and sound, its voyage
    closed and done,
From fearful trip the victor ship comes in with
    object won;
  Exult O shores, and ring O bells!
    But I, with mournful tread,
      Walk the deck my Captain lies,
        Fallen cold and dead.
                WALT WHITMAN.

Ingratitude.

"Ingratitude," by William Shakespeare (1564–1616), is an incisive
thrust at a refined vice.   It is a part of education to learn to be grateful.

    BLOW, blow, thou winter wind,
    Thou are not so unkind
      As man's ingratitude;
    Thy tooth is not so keen
    Because thou art not seen,
      Although thy breath be rude.

    Freeze, freeze, thou bitter sky,
    Thou dost not bite so nigh
      As benefits forgot;
    Though thou the waters warp,
    Thy sting is not so sharp
      As friend remembered not.
          WILLIAM SHAKESPEARE.

The Ivy Green.

"The Ivy Green," by Charles Dickens (1812–70), is a hardy poem in honour of a hardy plant. There is a wonderful ivy growing at Rhudlan, in northern Wales. Its roots are so large and strong that they form a comfortable seat for many persons, and no one can remember when they were smaller. This ivy envelops a great castle in ruins. Every child in that locality loves the old ivy. It is typical of the ivy as seen all through Wales and England.

O, A DAINTY plant is the ivy green,
   That creepeth o'er ruins old!
Of right choice food are his meals, I ween,
   In his cell so lone and cold.
The walls must be crumbled, the stones decayed,
   To pleasure his dainty whim;
And the mouldering dust that years have made
   Is a merry meal for him.
        Creeping where no life is seen,
        A rare old plant is the ivy green.

Fast he stealeth on, though he wears no wings,
   And a staunch old heart has he!
How closely he twineth, how tight he clings
   To his friend, the huge oak tree!
And slyly he traileth along the ground,
   And his leaves he gently waves,
And he joyously twines and hugs around
   The rich mould of dead men's graves.
        Creeping where no life is seen,
        A rare old plant is the ivy green.

Whole ages have fled, and their works decayed,
   And nations have scattered been;

But the stout old ivy shall never fade
    From its hale and hearty green.
The brave old plant in its lonely days
    Shall fatten upon the past;
For the stateliest building man can raise
    Is the ivy's food at last.
        Creeping where no life is seen,
        A rare old plant is the ivy green.
                CHARLES DICKENS.

The Noble Nature.

"The Noble Nature," by Ben Jonson (1574-1637), needs no plea. A small virtue well polished is better than none.

IT is not growing like a tree
In bulk doth make man better be;
Or standing long an oak, three hundred year,
To fall a log at last, dry, bald, and sear
        A lily of a day
        Is fairer far in May,
     Although it fall and die that night,—
    It was the plant and flower of light.
In small proportions we just beauties see;
And in short measures life may perfect be.
                BEN JONSON.

The Flying Squirrel.

"The Flying Squirrel" is an honest account of a live creature that won his way into scores of hearts by his mad pranks and affectionate ways. It is enough that John Burroughs has commended the poem.

OF all the woodland creatures,
    The quaintest little sprite

Is the dainty flying squirrel
  In vest of shining white,
In coat of silver gray,
  And vest of shining white.

His furry Quaker jacket
  Is trimmed with stripe of black;
A furry plume to match it
  Is curling o'er his back;
New curved with every motion,
  His plume curls o'er his back.

No little new-born baby
  Has pinker feet than he;
Each tiny toe is cushioned
  With velvet cushions three;
Three wee, pink, velvet cushions
  Almost too small to see.

Who said, "The foot of baby
  Might tempt an angel's kiss"?
I know a score of school-boys
  Who put their lips to this,—
This wee foot of the squirrel,
  And left a loving kiss.

The tiny thief has hidden
  My candy and my plum;
Ah, there he comes unbidden
  To gently nip my thumb,—
Down in his home (my pocket)
  He gently nips my thumb.

How strange the food he covets,
  The restless, restless wight;—
Fred's old stuffed armadillo
  He found a tempting bite,
Fred's old stuffed armadillo,
  With ears a perfect fright.

The Lady Ruth's great bureau,
  Each foot a dragon's paw!
The midget ate the nails from
  His famous antique claw.
Oh, what a cruel beastie
  To hurt a dragon's claw!

To autographic copies
  Upon my choicest shelf,—
To every dainty volume
  The rogue has helped himself.
My books! Oh dear! No matter!
  The rogue has helped himself.

And yet, my little squirrel,
  Your taste is not so bad;
You've swallowed Caird completely
  And psychologic Ladd.
Rosmini you've digested,
  And Kant in rags you've clad.

Gnaw on, my elfish rodent!
  Lay all the sages low!
My pretty lace and ribbons,
  They're yours for weal or woe!
My pocket-book's in tatters
  Because you like it so.

                              MARY E. BURT.

Warren's Address to the American Soldiers.

There is never a boy who objects to learning "Warren's Address," by John Pierpont (1785-1866). To stand by one's own rights is inherent in every true American. This poem is doubtless developed from Robert Burns's "Bannockburn." (1785-1866.)

STAND! the ground's your own, my braves!
Will ye give it up to slaves?
Will ye look for greener graves?
   Hope ye mercy still?
What's the mercy despots feel?
Hear it in that battle-peal!
Read it on yon bristling steel!
   Ask it,—ye who will.

Fear ye foes who kill for hire?
Will ye to your homes retire?
Look behind you! they're afire!
   And, before you, see
Who have done it!—From the vale
On they come!—And will ye quail?—
Leaden rain and iron hail
   Let their welcome be!

In the God of battles trust!
Die we may,—and die we must;
But, O, where can dust to dust
   Be consigned so well,
As where Heaven its dews shall shed
On the martyred patriot's bed,
And the rocks shall raise their head,
   Of his deeds to tell!

                JOHN PIERPONT.

The Song in Camp.

"The Song in Camp" is Bayard Taylor's best effort as far as young boys and girls are concerned. It is a most valuable poem. I once heard a clergyman in Chicago use it as a text for his sermon. Since then "Annie Laurie" has become the song of the Labour party. "The Song in Camp" voices a universal feeling. (1825–78.)

"Give us a song!" the soldiers cried,
    The outer trenches guarding,
When the heated guns of the camps allied
    Grew weary of bombarding.

The dark Redan, in silent scoff,
    Lay, grim and threatening, under;
And the tawny mound of the Malakoff
    No longer belched its thunder.

There was a pause. A guardsman said,
    "We storm the forts to-morrow;
Sing while we may, another day
    Will bring enough of sorrow."

They lay along the battery's side,
    Below the smoking cannon:
Brave hearts, from Severn and from Clyde,
    And from the banks of Shannon.

They sang of love, and not of fame;
    Forgot was Britain's glory:
Each heart recalled a different name,
    But all sang "Annie Laurie."

Voice after voice caught up the song,
  Until its tender passion
Rose like an anthem, rich and strong,—
  Their battle-eve confession.

Dear girl, her name he dared not speak,
  But, as the song grew louder,
Something upon the soldier's cheek
  Washed off the stains of powder.

Beyond the darkening ocean burned
  The bloody sunset's embers,
While the Crimean valleys learned
  How English love remembers.

And once again a fire of hell
  Rained on the Russian quarters,
With scream of shot, and burst of shell,
  And bellowing of the mortars!

And Irish Nora's eyes are dim
  For a singer, dumb and gory;
And English Mary mourns for him
  Who sang of "Annie Laurie."

Sleep, soldiers! still in honoured rest
  Your truth and valour wearing:
The bravest are the tenderest,—
  The loving are the daring.

BAYARD TAYLOR.

The Bugle Song.

"The Bugle Song" (by Alfred Tennyson, 1809–90), says Heydrick, "has for its central theme the undying power of human love. The music is notable for sweetness and delicacy."

THE splendour falls on castle walls
 And snowy summits old in story:
The long light shakes across the lakes
 And the wild cataract leaps in glory.
Blow, bugle, blow, set the wild echoes flying,
Blow, bugle; answer, echoes, dying, dying, dying.

O hark, O hear! how thin and clear,
 And thinner, clearer, farther going!
O sweet and far from cliff and scar
 The horns of Elfland faintly blowing!
Blow, let us hear the purple glens replying:
Blow, bugle; answer, echoes, dying, dying, dying.

O love, they die in yon rich sky,
 They faint on hill or field or river:
Our echoes roll from soul to soul,
 And grow forever and forever.
Blow, bugle, blow, set the wild echoes flying,
And answer, echoes, answer, dying, dying, dying.
ALFRED TENNYSON.

The " Three Bells " of Glasgow.

"The Three Bells of Glasgow," by Whittier (1807–92), cannot be praised too highly for its ethical value. Children always love to learn it after hearing it read correctly and by one who understands and appreciates it. "Stand by" is the motto. My pupils teach it to me once a year and learn it themselves, too.

BENEATH the low-hung night cloud
    That raked her splintering mast
The good ship settled slowly,
    The cruel leak gained fast.

Over the awful ocean
    Her signal guns pealed out.
Dear God! was that Thy answer
    From the horror round about?

A voice came down the wild wind,
    "Ho! ship ahoy!" its cry:
"Our stout *Three Bells* of Glasgow
    Shall stand till daylight by!"

Hour after hour crept slowly,
    Yet on the heaving swells
Tossed up and down the ship-lights,
    The lights of the *Three Bells!*

And ship to ship made signals,
    Man answered back to man,
While oft, to cheer and hearten,
    The *Three Bells* nearer ran:

And the captain from her taffrail
    Sent down his hopeful cry.
"Take heart! Hold on!" he shouted.
    "The *Three Bells* shall stand by!"

All night across the waters
  The tossing lights shone clear;
All night from reeling taffrail
  The *Three Bells* sent her cheer.

And when the dreary watches
  Of storm and darkness passed,
Just as the wreck lurched under,
  All souls were saved at last.

Sail on, *Three Bells*, forever,
  In grateful memory sail!
Ring on, *Three Bells* of rescue,
  Above the wave and gale!

Type of the Love eternal,
  Repeat the Master's cry,
As tossing through our darkness
  The lights of God draw nigh!
                    JOHN G. WHITTIER.

Sheridan's Ride.

There never was a boy who did not like "Sheridan's Ride," by T. Buchanan Read (1822–72). The swing and gallop in it take every boy off from his feet. The children never teach this poem to me, because they love to learn it at first sight. It is easily memorised.

Up from the South at break of day,
Bringing to Winchester fresh dismay,
The affrighted air with a shudder bore,
Like a herald in haste, to the chieftain's door,
The terrible grumble, and rumble, and roar,
Telling the battle was on once more,
And Sheridan twenty miles away.

And wider still those billows of war
Thundered along the horizon's bar;
And louder yet into Winchester rolled
The roar of that red sea uncontrolled,
Making the blood of the listener cold
As he thought of the stake in that fiery fray,
And Sheridan twenty miles away.

But there is a road from Winchester town,
A good, broad highway leading down;
And there, through the flush of the morning light,
A steed as black as the steeds of night
Was seen to pass as with eagle flight;
As if he knew the terrible need,
He stretched away with his utmost speed;
Hills rose and fell; but his heart was gay,
With Sheridan fifteen miles away.

Still sprung from those swift hoofs, thundering
    South,
The dust, like smoke from the cannon's mouth;
Or the trail of a comet, sweeping faster and faster,
Foreboding to traitors the doom of disaster.
The heart of the steed and the heart of the master
Were beating like prisoners assaulting their walls,
Impatient to be where the battle-field calls;
Every nerve of the charger was strained to full play,
With Sheridan only ten miles away.

Under his spurning feet the road
Like an arrowy Alpine river flowed,
And the landscape sped away behind
Like an ocean flying before the wind,

And the steed, like a bark fed with furnace fire,
Swept on, with his wild eye full of ire.
But lo! he is nearing his heart's desire;
He is snuffing the smoke of the roaring fray,
With Sheridan only five miles away.

The first that the General saw were the groups
Of stragglers, and then the retreating troops.
What was done—what to do? A glance told him
    both,
Then striking his spurs, with a terrible oath,
He dashed down the line, mid a storm of huzzas,
And the wave of retreat checked its course there,
    because
The sight of the master compelled it to pause.
With foam and with dust the black charger was
    gray;
By the flash of his eye, and the red nostrils' play,
He seemed to the whole great army to say:
"I have brought you Sheridan all the way
From Winchester down to save the day!"

Hurrah! hurrah for Sheridan!
Hurrah! hurrah for horse and man!
And when their statues are placed on high,
Under the dome of the Union sky,
The American soldiers' Temple of Fame,
There with the glorious General's name
Be it said, in letters both bold and bright:
"Here is the steed that saved the day,
By carrying Sheridan into the fight
From Winchester, twenty miles away!"

                          THOMAS BUCHANAN READ.

The Sandpiper.

"The Sandpiper," by Celia Thaxter (1836-94), is placed here because a goodly percentage of the children who read it want to learn it.

ACROSS the lonely beach we flit,
  One little sandpiper and I,
And fast I gather, bit by bit,
  The scattered driftwood, bleached and dry.
The wild waves reach their hands for it,
  The wild wind raves, the tide runs high,
As up and down the beach we flit,
  One little sandpiper and I.

Above our heads the sullen clouds
  Scud, black and swift, across the sky;
Like silent ghosts in misty shrouds
  Stand out the white lighthouses high.
Almost as far as eye can reach
  I see the close-reefed vessels fly,
As fast we flit along the beach,
  One little sandpiper and I.

I watch him as he skims along,
  Uttering his sweet and mournful crv:
He starts not at my fitful song,
  Nor flash of fluttering drapery.
He has no thought of any wrong,
  He scans me with a fearless eye;
Stanch friends are we, well tried and strong,
  The little sandpiper and I.

Comrade, where wilt thou be to-night,
  When the loosed storm breaks furiously?

My driftwood fire will burn so bright!
　To what warm shelter canst thou fly?
I do not fear for thee, though wroth
　The tempest rushes through the sky;
For are we not God's children both,
　Thou, little sandpiper, and I?

CELIA THAXTER.

Lady Clare.

Girls always love "Lady Clare" and "The Lord of Burleigh." They like to think that it is enough to be a splendid woman without title or wealth. They want to be loved, if they are loved at all, for their good hearts and graces of mind. Tennyson (1809–92) makes this point repeatedly through his poems.

IT was the time when lilies blow
　And clouds are highest up in air;
Lord Ronald brought a lily-white doe
　To give his cousin, Lady Clare.

I trow they did not part in scorn:
　Lovers long-betroth'd were they:
They too will wed the morrow morn:
　God's blessing on the day!

"He does not love me for my birth,
　Nor for my lands so broad and fair;
He loves me for my own true worth,
　And that is well," said Lady Clare.

In there came old Alice the nurse;
　Said: "Who was this that went from **thee?**"
"It was my cousin," said Lady Clare;
　"**To-morrow** he weds with me."

"O God be thank'd!" said Alice the nurse,
  "That all comes round so just and fair:
Lord Ronald is heir of all your lands,
  And you are not the Lady Clare."

"Are ye out of your mind, my nurse, my nurse,"
  Said Lady Clare, "that ye speak so wild?"
"As God's above," said Alice the nurse,
  "I speak the truth: you are my child.

"The old Earl's daughter died at my breast;
  I speak the truth, as I live by bread!
I buried her like my own sweet child,
  And put my child in her stead."

"Falsely, falsely have ye done,
  O mother," she said, "if this be true,
To keep the best man under the sun
  So many years from his due."

"Nay now, my child," said Alice the nurse,
  "But keep the secret for your life,
And all you have will be Lord Ronald's
  When you are man and wife."

"If I'm a beggar born," she said,
  "I will speak out, for I dare not lie.
Pull off, pull off the brooch of gold,
  And fling the diamond necklace by."

"Nay now, my child," said Alice the nurse,
  "But keep the secret all ye can."
She said: "Not so: but I will know
  If there be any faith in man."

"Nay now, what faith?" said Alice the nurse;
  "The man will cleave unto his right."
"And he shall have it," the lady replied,
  "Tho' I should die to-night."

"Yet give one kiss to your mother dear!
  Alas! my child, I sinn'd for thee."
"O mother, mother, mother," she said,
  "So strange it seems to me.

"Yet here's a kiss for my mother dear,
  My mother dear, if this be so,
And lay your hand upon my head,
  And bless me, mother, ere I go."

She clad herself in a russet gown,
  She was no longer Lady Clare:
She went by dale, and she went by down,
  With a single rose in her hair.

The lily-white doe Lord Ronald had brought
  Leapt up from where she lay,
Dropt her head in the maiden's hand,
  And follow'd her all the way.

Down stept Lord Ronald from his tower:
  "O Lady Clare, you shame your worth!
Why come you drest like a village maid,
  That are the flower of the earth?"

"If I come drest like a village maid,
  I am but as my fortunes are:
I am a beggar born," she said,
  "And not the Lady Clare."

"Play me no tricks," said Lord Ronald,
  "For I am yours in word and in deed.
Play me no tricks," said Lord Ronald,
  "Your riddle is hard to read."

O and proudly stood she up!
  Her heart within her did not fail:
She look'd into Lord Ronald's eyes,
  And told him all her nurse's tale.

He laugh'd a laugh of merry scorn:
  He turn'd and kiss'd her where she stood:
"If you are not the heiress born,
  And I," said he, "the next in blood—

"If you are not the heiress born,
  And I," said he, "the lawful heir,
We two will wed to-morrow morn,
  And you shall still be Lady Clare."
               ALFRED TENNYSON.

The Lord of Burleigh.

In her ear he whispers gaily,
  "If my heart by signs can tell,
Maiden, I have watched thee daily,
  And I think thou lov'st me well."
She replies, in accents fainter,
  "There is none I love like thee."
He is but a landscape-painter,
  And a village maiden she.

He to lips, that fondly falter,
  Presses his without reproof;
Leads her to the village altar,
  And they leave her father's roof.

"I can make no marriage present;
  Little can I give my wife.
Love will make our cottage pleasant,
  And I love thee more than life."

They by parks and lodges going
  See the lordly castles stand;
Summer woods, about them blowing,
  Made a murmur in the land.

From deep thought himself he rouses,
  Says to her that loves him well,
"Let us see these handsome houses
  Where the wealthy nobles dwell."

So she goes by him attended,
  Hears him lovingly converse,
Sees whatever fair and splendid
  Lay betwixt his home and hers.
Parks with oak and chestnut shady,
  Parks and order'd gardens great,
Ancient homes of lord and lady,
  Built for pleasure and for state.

All he shows her makes him dearer;
  Evermore she seems to gaze
On that cottage growing nearer,
  Where they twain will spend their days.

O but she will love him truly!
  He shall have a cheerful home;
She will order all things duly
  When beneath his roof they come.

Thus her heart rejoices greatly
  Till a gateway she discerns
With armorial bearings stately,
  And beneath the gate she turns;
Sees a mansion more majestic
  Than all those she saw before;
Many a gallant gay domestic
  Bows before him at the door.

And they speak in gentle murmur
  When they answer to his call,
While he treads with footstep firmer,
  Leading on from hall to hall.

And while now she wanders blindly,
  Nor the meaning can divine,
Proudly turns he round and kindly,
  "All of this is mine and thine."

Here he lives in state and bounty,
  Lord of Burleigh, fair and free.
Not a lord in all the county
  Is so great a lord as he.
All at once the colour flushes
  Her sweet face from brow to chin;
As it were with shame she blushes,
  And her spirit changed within.

Then her countenance all over
　　Pale again as death did prove:
But he clasp'd her like a lover,
　　And he cheer'd her soul with love.

So she strove against her weakness,
　　Tho' at times her spirits sank;
Shaped her heart with woman's meekness
　　To all duties of her rank;
And a gentle consort made he,
　　And her gentle mind was such
That she grew a noble lady,
　　And the people loved her much.
But a trouble weigh'd upon her
　　And perplex'd her, night and morn,
With the burden of an honour
　　Unto which she was not born.

Faint she grew and ever fainter,
　　As she murmur'd, "Oh, that he
Were once more that landscape-painter
　　Which did win my heart from me!"

So she droop'd and droop'd before him,
　　Fading slowly from his side;
Three fair children first she bore him,
　　Then before her time she died.

Weeping, weeping late and early,
　　Walking up and pacing down,
Deeply mourn'd the Lord of Burleigh,
　　Burleigh-house by Stamford-town

And he came to look upon her,
  And he look'd at her and said,
"Bring the dress and put it on her
  That she wore when she was wed."

Then her people, softly treading,
  Bore to earth her body, drest
In the dress that she was wed in,
  That her spirit might have rest.

ALFRED TENNYSON.

Hiawatha's Childhood.

"Hiawatha" needs no commendation. Hundreds of thousands of children in our land know snatches of it. It is a child's poem, every line of it. One summer in Boston more than 50,000 people went to take a peep at the poet's house. (1807–82.)

By the shores of Gitche Gumee,
By the shining Big-Sea-Water,
Stood the wigwam of Nokomis,
Daughter of the Moon, Nokomis.
Dark behind it rose the forest,
Rose the black and gloomy pine-trees,
Rose the firs with cones upon them;
Bright before it beat the water,
Beat the clear and sunny water,
Beat the shining Big-Sea-Water.

There the wrinkled old Nokomis
Nursed the little Hiawatha,
Rocked him in his linden cradle,
Bedded soft in moss and rushes,
Safely bound with reindeer sinews;

Stilled his fretful wail by saying,
"Hush! the Naked Bear will hear thee!"
Lulled him into slumber, singing,
"Ewa-yea! my little owlet!
Who is this that lights the wigwam?
With his great eyes lights the wigwam?
Ewa-yea! my little owlet!"

Many things Nokomis taught him
Of the stars that shine in heaven;
Showed him Ishkoodah, the comet,
Ishkoodah, with fiery tresses;
Showed the Death-Dance of the spirits,
Warriors with their plumes and war-clubs,
Flaring far away to northward
In the frosty nights of winter;
Showed the broad, white road in heaven,
Pathway of the ghosts, the shadows,
Running straight across the heavens,
Crowded with the ghosts, the shadows.

At the door, on summer evenings,
Sat the little Hiawatha;
Heard the whispering of the pine-trees,
Heard the lapping of the water,
Sounds of music, words of wonder;
"Minnie-wawa!" said the pine-trees,
"Mudway-aushka!" said the water;
Saw the fire-fly, Wah-wah-taysee,
Flitting through the dusk of evening,
With the twinkle of its candle
Lighting up the brakes and bushes,
And he sang the song of children,

Sang the song Nokomis taught him:
"Wah-wah-taysee, little fire-fly,
Little, flitting, white-fire insect,
Little, dancing, white-fire creature,
Light me with your little candle,
Ere upon my bed I lay me,
Ere in sleep I close my eyelids!"

Saw the moon rise from the water
Rippling, rounding from the water,
Saw the flecks and shadows on it,
Whispered, "What is that, Nokomis?"
And the good Nokomis answered:
"Once a warrior, very angry,
Seized his grandmother, and threw her
Up into the sky at midnight;
Right against the moon he threw her;
'Tis her body that you see there."

Saw the rainbow in the heaven,
In the eastern sky, the rainbow,
Whispered, "What is that, Nokomis?"
And the good Nokomis answered:
"'Tis the heaven of flowers you see there;
All the wild-flowers of the forest,
All the lilies of the prairie,
When on earth they fade and perish,
Blossom in that heaven above us."

When he heard the owls at midnight,
Hooting, laughing in the forest,
"What is that?" he cried, in terror;
"What is that," he said, "Nokomis?"

And the good Nokomis answered:
"That is but the owl and owlet,
Talking in their native language,
Talking, scolding at each other."

Then the little Hiawatha
Learned of every bird its language,
Learned their names and all their secrets,
How they built their nests in summer,
Where they hid themselves in winter,
Talked with them whene'er he met them,
Called them "Hiawatha's Chickens."

Of all beasts he learned the language,
Learned their names and all their secrets,
How the beavers built their lodges,
Where the squirrels hid their acorns,
How the reindeer ran so swiftly,
Why the rabbit was so timid,
Talked with them whene'er he met them,
Called them "Hiawatha's Brothers."

HENRY W. LONGFELLOW.

I Wandered Lonely as a Cloud.

"The Daffodil" is here out of compliment to a splendid school and a splendid teacher at Poughkeepsie. I found the pupils learning the poem, the teacher having placed a bunch of daffodils in a vase before them. It was a charming lesson. (1770-96.)

I WANDERED lonely as a cloud
    That floats on high o'er vales and hills,
When all at once I saw a crowd,
    A host of golden daffodils:
Beside the lake, beneath the trees,
Fluttering and dancing in the breeze.

Continuous as the stars that shine
   And twinkle on the milky way,
They stretched in never-ending line
   Along the margin of a bay:
Ten thousand saw I at a glance,
Tossing their heads in sprightly dance.

The waves beside them danced, but they
   Outdid the sparkling waves in glee:—
A poet could not but be gay
   In such a jocund company;
I gazed—and gazed—but little thought
What wealth the show to me had brought.

For oft, when on my couch I lie
   In vacant or in pensive mood,
They flash upon that inward eye
   Which is the bliss of solitude;
And then my heart with pleasure fills,
And dances with the daffodils.

             WILLIAM WORDSWORTH.

John Barleycorn.

"John Barleycorn" is a favourite with boys because it pictures a successful struggle. One editor has made a temperance poem of it, mistaking its true intent. The poem is a strong expression of a plowman's love for a hardy, food-giving grain which has sprung to life through his efforts. (1759–96.)

THERE were three kings into the East,
   Three kings both great and high;
And they ha'e sworn a solemn oath
   John Barleycorn should die.

They took a plow and plowed him down,
  Put clods upon his head;
And they ha'e sworn a solemn oath
  John Barleycorn was dead.

But the cheerful spring came kindly on,
  And showers began to fall;
John Barleycorn got up again,
  And sore surprised them all.

The sultry suns of summer came,
  And he grew thick and strong;
His head well arm'd wi' pointed spears,
  That no one should him wrong.

The sober autumn entered mild,
  And he grew wan and pale;
His bending joints and drooping head
  Showed he began to fail.

His colour sickened more and more,
  He faded into age;
And then his enemies began
  To show their deadly rage.

They took a weapon long and sharp,
  And cut him by the knee;
Then tied him fast upon a cart,
  Like a rogue for forgery.

They laid him down upon his back,
  And cudgelled him full sore;
They hung him up before the storm,
  And turn'd him o'er and o'er.

They filled up then a darksome pit
  With water to the brim,
And heaved in poor John Barleycorn,
  To let him sink or swim.

They laid him out upon the floor,
  To work him further woe;
And still as signs of life appeared,
  They tossed him to and fro.

They wasted o'er a scorching flame
  The marrow of his bones;
But a miller used him worst of all—
  He crushed him 'tween two stones.

And they have taken his very heart's blood,
  And drunk it round and round;
And still the more and more they drank,
  Their joy did more abound.

                                    ROBERT BURNS.

A Life on the Ocean Wave.

"A Life on the Ocean Wave," by Epes Sargent (1813–80), gives
the swing and motion of the water of the great ocean. Children
remember it almost unconsciously after hearing it read several times.

A LIFE on the ocean wave,
  A home on the rolling deep,
Where the scattered waters rave,
  And the winds their revels keep!
Like an eagle caged, I pine
  On this dull, unchanging shore:
Oh! give me the flashing brine,
  The spray and the tempest's roar!

Once more on the deck I stand
    Of my own swift-gliding craft:
Set sail! farewell to the land!
    The gale follows fair abaft.
We shoot through the sparkling foam
    Like an ocean-bird set free;—
Like the ocean-bird, our home
    We'll find far out on the sea.

The land is no longer in view,
    The clouds have begun to frown;
But with a stout vessel and crew,
    We'll say, Let the storm come down!
And the song of our hearts shall be,
    While the winds and the waters rave,
A home on the rolling sea!
    A life on the ocean wave!

EPES SARGENT.

The Death of the Old Year.

It is customary, every New Year's eve in America, to ring bells, fire guns, send up rockets, and, in many other ways, to show joy and gratitude that the old year has been so kind, and that the new year is so auspicious. The emphasis in Tennyson's poem is laid on gratitude for past benefits so easily forgotten rather than upon the possible advantages of the unknown and untried future.

FULL knee-deep lies the winter snow,
And the winter winds are wearily sighing:
Toll ye the church-bell sad and slow,
And tread softly and speak low,
For the old year lies a-dying.
        Old year, you must not die;
        You came to us so readily,

You lived with us so steadily,
Old year, you shall not die.

He lieth still: he doth not move:
He will not see the dawn of day.
He hath no other life above.
He gave me a friend, and a true true-love,
And the New-year will take 'em away.
Old year, you must not go;
So long as you have been with us,
Such joy as you have seen with us,
Old year, you shall not go.

He froth'd his bumpers to the brim;
A jollier year we shall not see.
But tho' his eyes are waxing dim,
And tho' his foes speak ill of him,
He was a friend to me.
Old year, you shall not die;
We did so laugh and cry with you,
I've half a mind to die with you,
Old year, if you must die.

He was full of joke and jest,
But all his merry quips are o'er.
To see him die, across the waste
His son and heir doth ride post-haste,
But he'll be dead before.
Every one for his own.
The night is starry and cold, my friend,
And the New-year blithe and bold, my
friend,
Comes up to take his own.

How hard he breathes! over the snow
I heard just now the crowing cock.
The shadows flicker to and fro:
The cricket chirps: the light burns low:
'Tis nearly twelve o'clock.
> Shake hands, before you die.
> Old year, we'll dearly rue for you:
> What is it we can do for you?
> Speak out before you die.

His face is growing sharp and thin.
Alack! our friend is gone.
Close up his eyes: tie up his chin:
Step from the corpse, and let him in
That standeth there alone,
> And waiteth at the door.
> There's a new foot on the floor, my friend
> And a new face at the door, my friend,
> A new face at the door.
>> ALFRED TENNYSON.

Abou Ben Adhem.

"Abou Ben Adhem" has won its way to the popular heart because the "Brotherhood of Man" is the motto of this age. (1784–1859.)

ABOU BEN ADHEM (may his tribe increase!)
Awoke one night from a deep dream of peace,
And saw within the moonlight in his room,
Making it rich and like a lily in bloom,
An angel writing in a book of gold.

Exceeding peace had made Ben Adhem bold;
And to the presence in the room he said,
"What writest thou?" The vision raised its head,
And, with a look made of all sweet accord,
Answered, "The names of those who love the
    Lord."

"And is mine one?" said Abou. "Nay, not so,"
Replied the angel. Abou spoke more low,
But cheerly still; and said, "I pray thee, then,
Write me as one that loves his fellow-men."

The angel wrote, and vanished. The next night
It came again, with a great wakening light,
And showed the names whom love of God had
    blessed;
And, lo! Ben Adhem's name led all the rest.

                                    LEIGH HUNT.

Farm-Yard Song.

"A Farm-Yard Song" was popular years ago with Burbank, the great reader. How the boys and girls loved it! The author, J. T. Trowbridge (1827–still living), "is a boy-hearted man," says John Burroughs. The poem is just as popular as it ever was.

OVER the hill the farm-boy goes,
His shadow lengthens along the land,
A giant staff in a giant hand;
In the poplar-tree, above the spring,
The katydid begins to sing;
      The early dews are falling;—
Into the stone-heap darts the mink;
The swallows skim the river's brink;
And home to the woodland fly the crows,
When over the hill the farm-boy goes,
      Cheerily calling,—
  "Co', boss! co', boss! co'! co'! co'!"
Farther, farther over the hill,
Faintly calling, calling still,—
  "Co', boss! co', boss! co'! co'!"

Into the yard the farmer goes,
With grateful heart, at the close of day;
Harness and chain are hung away;
In the wagon-shed stand yoke and plow;
The straw's in the stack, the hay in the mow,
      The cooling dews are falling;—
The friendly sheep his welcome bleat,
The pigs come grunting to his feet,
The whinnying mare her master knows,
When into the yard the farmer goes,
      His cattle calling,—
  "Co', boss! co', boss! co'! co'! co'!"

While still the cow-boy, far away,
Goes seeking those that have gone astray,—
  "Co', boss! co', boss! co'! co'!"

Now to her task the milkmaid goes.
The cattle come crowding through the gate,
Lowing, pushing, little and great;
About the trough, by the farm-yard pump,
The frolicsome yearlings frisk and jump,
    · While the pleasant dews are falling;—
The new-milch heifer is quick and shy,
But the old cow waits with tranquil eye;
And the white stream into the bright pail flows,
When to her task the milkmaid goes,
    Soothingly calling,—
  "So, boss! so, boss! so! so! so!"
The cheerful milkmaid takes her stool,
And sits and milks in the twilight cool,
  Saying, "So! so, boss! so! so!"

To supper at last the farmer goes.
The apples are pared, the paper read,
The stories are told, then all to bed.
Without, the crickets' ceaseless song
Makes shrill the silence all night long;
    The heavy dews are falling.
The housewife's hand has turned the lock;
Drowsily ticks the kitchen clock;
The household sinks to deep repose;
But still in sleep the farm-boy goes
    Singing, calling,—
  "Co', boss! co', boss! co'! co'! co'!"

And oft the milkmaid, in her dreams,
Drums in the pail with the flashing streams,
   Murmuring, "So, boss! so!"

                    J. T. TROWBRIDGE.

To a Mouse,

ON TURNING UP HER NEST WITH THE PLOW,
NOVEMBER, 1785

"To a Mouse" and "To a Mountain Daisy," by Robert Burns (1759-
96), are the ineffable touches of tenderness that illumine the sturdy plow-
man. The contrast between the strong man and the delicate flower or
creature at his mercy makes tenderness in man a vital point in char-
acter.

[The lines "To a Mouse" seem by report to have
been composed while Burns was actually plowing.
One of the poet's first editors wrote: "John
Blane, who had acted as gaudsman to Burns, and
who lived sixty years afterward, had a distinct
recollection of the turning up of the mouse. Like
a thoughtless youth as he was, he ran after the
creature to kill it, but was checked and recalled
by his master, who he observed became thereafter
thoughtful and abstracted. Burns, who treated
his servants with the familiarity of fellow-labourers,
soon afterward read the poem to Blane."

   WEE, sleekit, cow'rin', tim'rous beastie,
   Oh, what a panic's in thy breastie!
   Thou needna start awa' sae hasty,
         Wi' bickering brattle!
   I wad be laith to rin and chase thee,
         Wi' murd'ring pattle!

I'm truly sorry man's dominion
Has broken Nature's social union,
And justifies that ill opinion,
    Which makes thee startle
At me, thy poor earth-born companion
    And fellow-mortal!

I doubtna, whiles, but thou may thieve;
What then? poor beastie, thou maun live!
A daimen icker in a thrave
    'S a sma' request:
I'll get a blessin' wi' the lave,
    And never miss 't!

Thy wee bit housie, too, in ruin!
Its silly wa's the win's are strewin'!
And naething now to big a new ane
    O' foggage green,
And bleak December's winds ensuin',
    Baith snell and keen!

Thou saw the fields laid bare and waste,
And weary winter comin' fast,
And cozie here, beneath the blast,
    Thou thought to dwell,
Till, crash! the cruel coulter passed
    Out through thy cell.

That wee bit heap o' leaves and stibble
Has cost thee monie a weary nibble!
Now thou's turned out for a' thy trouble,
    But house or hald,
To thole the winter's sleety dribble,
    And cranreuch cauld!

But, Mousie, thou art no thy lane,
In proving foresight may be vain:
The best-laid schemes o' mice and men
    Gang aft a-gley,
And lea'e us naught but grief and pain,
    For promised joy.

Still thou art blest, compared wi' me!
The present only toucheth thee:
But, och! I backward cast my e'e
    On prospects drear!
And forward, though I canna see,
    I guess and fear.

                ROBERT BURNS.

To a Mountain Daisy,

ON TURNING ONE DOWN WITH THE PLOW IN APRIL, 1786

WEE, modest, crimson-tippèd flower,
Thou 's met me in an evil hour;
For I maun crush amang the stoure
    Thy slender stem:
To spare thee now is past my power,
    Thou bonny gem.

Alas! it's no thy neebor sweet,
The bonny lark, companion meet,
Bending thee 'mang the dewy weet,
    Wi' speckled breast,
When upward-springing, blithe, to greet
    The purpling east!

Cauld blew the bitter biting north
Upon thy early, humble birth;
Yet cheerfully thou glinted forth
        Amid the storm,
Scarce reared above the parent earth
        Thy tender form.

The flaunting flowers our gardens yield,
High sheltering woods and wa's maun shield,
But thou, beneath the random bield
        O' clod or stane,
Adorns the histie stibble-field,
        Unseen, alane.

There, in thy scanty mantle clad,
Thy snawie bosom sunward spread,
Thou lifts thy unassuming head
        In humble guise;
But now the share uptears thy bed,
        And low thou lies!

Such is the fate of artless maid,
Sweet floweret of the rural shade!
By love's simplicity betrayed,
        And guileless trust,
Till she, like thee, all soiled, is laid
        Low i' the dust.

Such is the fate of simple bard,
On life's rough ocean luckless starr'd!
Unskilful he to note the card
        Of prudent lore,
Till billows rage, and gales blow hard,
        And whelm him o'er!

Such fate to suffering worth is given,
Who long with wants and woes has striven,
By human pride or cunning driven
      To misery's brink,
Till wrenched of every stay but Heaven,
      He, ruined, sink!

Even thou who mourn'st the Daisy's fate,
That fate is thine—no distant date;
Stern Ruin's plowshare drives, elate,
      Full on thy bloom,
Till crushed beneath the furrow's weight
      Shall be thy doom.

                    ROBERT BURNS.

Barbara Frietchie.

"Barbara Frietchie" will be beloved of all times because she was an old woman (not necessarily an old lady) *worthy of her years.* Old age is honourable if it carries a head that has a halo. (1807-92.)

Up from the meadows rich with corn,
Clear in the cool September morn,

The clustered spires of Frederick stand
Green-walled by the hills of Maryland.

Round about them orchards sweep,
Apple and peach tree fruited deep,

Fair as the garden of the Lord
To the eyes of the famished rebel horde,

On that pleasant morn of the early fall
When Lee marched over the mountain-wall,—

Over the mountains winding down,
Horse and foot, into Frederick town.

Forty flags with their silver stars,
Forty flags with their crimson bars,

Flapped in the morning wind: the sun
Of noon looked down, and saw not one.

Up rose old Barbara Frietchie then,
Bowed with her fourscore years and ten;

Bravest of all in Frederick town,
She took up the flag the men hauled down;

In her attic window the staff she set,
To show that one heart was loyal yet.

Up the street came the rebel tread,
Stonewall Jackson riding ahead.

Under his slouched hat left and right
He glanced: the old flag met his sight.

"Halt!"—the dust-brown ranks stood fast.
"Fire!"—out blazed the rifle-blast.

It shivered the window, pane and sash;
It rent the banner with seam and gash.

Quick, as it fell, from the broken staff
Dame Barbara snatched the silken scarf.

She leaned far out on the window-sill,
And shook it forth with a royal will.

"Shoot, if you must, this old gray head,
But spare your country's flag," she said.

A shade of sadness, a blush of shame,
Over the face of the leader came;

The nobler nature within him stirred
To life at that woman's deed and word:

"Who touches a hair of yon gray head
Dies like a dog!   March on!" he said.

All day long through Frederick street
Sounded the tread of marching feet:

All day long that free flag tost
Over the heads of the rebel host.

Ever its torn folds rose and fell
On the loyal winds that loved it well;

And through the hill-gaps sunset light
Shone over it with a warm good-night.

Barbara Frietchie's work is o'er,
And the rebel rides on his raids no more.

Honour to her! and let a tear
Fall, for her sake, on Stonewall's bier.

Over Barbara Frietchie's grave,
Flag of Freedom and Union, wave!

Peace and order and beauty draw
Round thy symbol of light and law;

And ever the stars above look down
On thy stars below in Frederick town!
                    JOHN G. WHITTIER.

PART III.

The Day's at the Morn

PART III

Lochinvar.

"Lochinvar" and "Lord Ullin's Daughter," the first by Scott (1771–1832) and the second by Campbell (1777–1844), are companions in sentiment and equally popular with boys who love to win anything desirable by heroic effort.

OH, young Lochinvar is come out of the west.
Through all the wide Border his steed was the
    best,
And save his good broadsword he weapons had
    none;
He rode all unarmed, and he rode all alone.
So faithful in love, and so dauntless in war,
There never was knight like the young Lochinvar.

He stayed not for brake, and he stopped not for
    stone,
He swam the Eske River where ford there was
    none:
But ere he alighted at Netherby gate
The bride had consented, the gallant came late:
For a laggard in love, and a dastard in war
Was to wed the fair Ellen of brave Lochinvar.

So boldly he entered the Netherby Hall,
Among bridesmen and kinsmen and brothers and
    all:
Then spoke the bride's father, his hand on his
    sword
(For the poor craven bridegroom said never a
    word),

"Oh, come ye in peace here, or come ye in war,
Or to dance at our bridal, young Lord Lochinvar?"

"I long woo'd your daughter, my suit you denied;—
Love swells like the Solway, but ebbs like its
    tide—
And now am I come, with this lost love of mine,
To lead but one measure, drink one cup of wine.
There are maidens in Scotland more lovely by far,
That would gladly be bride to the young
    Lochinvar."

The bride kissed the goblet; the knight took it up;
He quaffed of the wine, and he threw down the
    cup.
She looked down to blush, and she looked up to
    sigh,
With a smile on her lips and a tear in her eye.
He took her soft hand ere her mother could
    bar,—
"Now tread we a measure!" said young Lochinvar.

So stately his form, and so lovely her face,
That never a hall such a galliard did grace;
While her mother did fret, and her father did
    fume,
And the bridegroom stood dangling his bonnet
    and plume,
And the bridemaidens whispered, "'Twere better
    by far
To have matched our fair cousin with young
    Lochinvar."

One touch to her hand, and one word in her ear,
When they reached the hall door, and the charger
    stood near;
So light to the croupe the fair lady he swung,
So light to the saddle before her he sprung!
"She is won! we are gone, over bank, bush, and
    scaur;
They'll have fleet steeds that follow," quoth
    young Lochinvar.

There was mounting 'mong Græmes of the Netherby
    clan;
Forsters, Fenwicks, and Musgraves, they rode and
    they ran:
There was racing and chasing, on Cannobie Lee,
But the lost bride of Netherby ne'er did they see.
So daring in love, and so dauntless in war,
Have ye e'er heard of gallant like young Lochinvar?

                    Sir Walter Scott.

Lord Ullin's Daughter.

A chieftain, to the Highlands bound,
  Cries, "Boatman, do not tarry!
And I'll give thee a silver pound,
  To row us o'er the ferry."

"Now who be ye, would cross Lochgyle,
  This dark and stormy water?"
"O, I'm the chief of Ulva's isle,
  And this Lord Ullin's daughter.

"And fast before her father's men
  Three days we've fled together,
For should he find us in the glen,
  My blood would stain the heather.

"His horsemen hard behind us ride;
  Should they our steps discover,
Then who will cheer my bonny bride
  When they have slain her lover?"

Outspoke the hardy Highland wight,
  "I'll go, my chief—I'm ready;
It is not for your silver bright,
  But for your winsome lady:

"And by my word! the bonny bird
  In danger shall not tarry;
So though the waves are raging white,
  I'll row you o'er the ferry."

By this the storm grew loud apace,
  The water-wraith was shrieking;
And in the scowl of heaven each face
  Grew dark as they were speaking.

But still as wilder blew the wind,
  And as the night grew drearer,
Adown the glen rode armèd men,
  Their trampling sounded nearer.

"O haste thee, haste!" the lady cries,
  "Though tempests round us gather;
I'll meet the raging of the skies,
  But not an angry father."

The boat has left a stormy land,
  A stormy sea before her,—
When, oh! too strong for human hand,
  The tempest gather'd o'er her.

And still they row'd amid the roar
  Of waters fast prevailing:
Lord Ullin reach'd that fatal shore,
  His wrath was changed to wailing.

For sore dismay'd, through storm and shade,
  His child he did discover:—
One lovely hand she stretch'd for aid,
  And one was round her lover.

"Come back! come back!" he cried in grief,
  "Across this stormy water:
And I'll forgive your Highland chief,
  My daughter!—oh my daughter!"

'Twas vain the loud waves lashed the shore,
  Return or aid preventing;—
The waters wild went o'er his child,—
  And he was left lamenting.

THOMAS CAMPBELL.

The Charge of the Light Brigade.

"The Charge of the Light Brigade" (1809–92) unlike "Casabianca" shows obedience under stern necessity. Obedience is the salvation of any army. John Burroughs says: "I never hear that poem but what it thrills me through and through."

HALF a league, half a league,
  Half a league onward,
All in the valley of Death
  Rode the six hundred.

"Forward, the Light Brigade!
Charge for the guns!" he said:
Into the valley of Death
  Rode the six hundred.

"Forward, the Light Brigade!"
Was there a man dismay'd?
Not tho' the soldier knew
  Some one had blunder'd:
Theirs not to make reply,
Theirs not to reason why,
Theirs but to do and die:
Into the valley of Death
  Rode the six hundred.

Cannon to right of them,
Cannon to left of them,
Cannon in front of them
  Volley'd and thunder'd;
Storm'd at with shot and shell,
Boldly they rode and well,
Into the jaws of Death,
Into the mouth of Hell
  Rode the six hundred.

Flash'd all their sabers bare,
Flash'd as they turn'd in air
Sab'ring the gunners there,
Charging an army, while
  All the world wonder'd:
Plunged in the battery-smoke
Right thro' the line they broke;

Cossack and Russian
Reel'd from the saber-stroke
  Shatter'd and sunder'd.
Then they rode back, but not
  Not the six hundred.

Cannon to right of them,
Cannon to left of them,
Cannon behind them
  Volleyed and thundered:
Stormed at with shot and shell,
While horse and hero fell,
They that had fought so well
Came through the jaws of death
Back from the mouth of hell,
All that was left of them—
  Left of six hundred.

When can their glory fade?
Oh, the wild charge they made!
  All the world wondered.
Honour the charge they made!
Honour the Light Brigade—
  Noble six hundred!

ALFRED TENNYSON.

The Tournament.

There are several of Sidney Lanier's (1842–81) poems that children love to learn. "Tampa Robins," "The Tournament" (Joust I.), "Barnacles," "The Song of the Chattahoochee," and "The First Steamboat Up the Alabama" are among them. At our "poetry contests" the children have plainly demonstrated that this great poet has reached his hand down to the youngest. The time will doubtless come when it will be a part of education to be acquainted with Lanier, as it is now to be acquainted with Longfellow or Tennyson.

I.

BRIGHT shone the lists, blue bent the skies,
　　And the knights still hurried amain
To the tournament under the ladies' eyes,
　　Where the jousters were Heart and Brain.

II.

Flourished the trumpets, entered Heart,
　　A youth in crimson and gold;
Flourished again; Brain stood apart,
　　Steel-armoured, dark and cold.

III.

Heart's palfrey caracoled gaily round,
　　Heart tra-li-ra'd merrily;
But Brain sat still, with never a sound,
　　So cynical-calm was he.

IV.

Heart's helmet-crest bore favours three
　　From his lady's white hand caught;
While Brain wore a plumeless casque; not he
　　Or favour gave or sought.

v.

The trumpet blew; Heart shot a glance
　To catch his lady's eye,
But **Brain** gazed straight ahead, his lance
　To aim more faithfully.

vi.

They charged, they struck; both fell, both bled;
　Brain rose again, ungloved;
Heart, dying, smiled and faintly said,
　"My love to my beloved."

Sidney Lanier.

The Wind and the Moon.

Little Laddie, do you remember learning "The Wind and the Moon"? You were eight or nine years old, and you shut your eyes and puffed out your cheeks when you came to the line "He blew and He blew." The saucy wind made a great racket and the calm moon never noticed it. That gave you a great deal of pleasure, didn't it? We did not care much for the noisy, conceited wind. (1824-.)

Said the Wind to the Moon, "I will blow you out;
　　　You stare
　　　In the air
　　　Like a ghost in a chair,
Always looking what I am about—
I hate to be watched; I'll blow you out."

The Wind blew hard, and out went the Moon.
　　　So, deep
　　　On a heap
　　　Of clouds to sleep,
Down lay the Wind, and slumbered soon,
Muttering low, "I've done for that Moon."

He turned in his bed; she was there again!
                    On high
                    In the sky,
                    With her one ghost eye,
The Moon shone white and alive and plain.
Said the Wind, "I will blow you out again."

The Wind blew hard, and the Moon grew dim.
                    "With my sledge,
                    And my wedge,
                    I have knocked off her edge!
If only I blow right fierce and grim,
The creature will soon be dimmer than dim."

He blew and he blew, and she thinned to a thread.
                    "One puff
                    More's enough
                    To blow her to snuff!
One good puff more where the last was bred,
And glimmer, glimmer, glum will go the thread."

He blew a great blast, and the thread was gone.
                    In the air
                    Nowhere
                    Was a moonbeam bare;
Far off and harmless the shy stars shone—
Sure and certain the Moon was gone!

The Wind he took to his revels once more;
                    On down,
                    In town,
                    Like a merry-mad clown,
He leaped and hallooed with whistle and roar—
"What's that?"   The glimmering thread once more!

He flew in a rage—he danced and blew;
        But in vain
        Was the pain
        Of his bursting brain;
For still the broader the Moon-scrap grew,
The broader he swelled his big cheeks and blew.

Slowly she grew—till she filled the night,
        And shone
        On her throne
        In the sky alone,
A matchless, wonderful silvery light,
Radiant and lovely, the queen of the night.

Said the Wind: "What a marvel of power am I!
        With my breath,
        Good faith!
        I blew her to death—
First blew her away right out of the sky—
Then blew her in; what strength have I!"

But the Moon she knew nothing about the affair;
        For high
        In the sky,
        With her one white eye,
Motionless, miles above the air,
She had never heard the great Wind blare.

                        GEORGE MACDONALD.

Jesus the Carpenter.

"Jesus the Carpenter"—"same trade as me"—strikes a high note in favour of honest toil. (1848-.)

"Isn't this Joseph's son?"—ay, it is He;
Joseph the carpenter—same trade as me—
I thought as I'd find it—I knew it was here—
    But my sight's getting queer.

I don't know right where as His shed must ha'
    stood—
But often, as I've been a-planing my wood,
I've took off my hat, just with thinking of He
    At the same work as me.

He warn't that set up that He couldn't stoop down
And work in the country for folks in the town;
And I'll warrant He felt a bit pride, like I've done,
    At a good job begun.

The parson he knows that I'll not make too free,
But on Sunday I feels as pleased as can be,
When I wears my clean smock, and sits in a pew,
    And has taught a few.

I think of as how not the parson hissen,
As is teacher and father and shepherd o' men,
Not he knows as much of the Lord in that shed,
    Where He earned His own bread.

And when I goes home to my missus, says she,
"Are ye wanting your key?"
For she knows my queer ways, and my love for
    the shed
    (We've been forty years wed).

So I comes right away by mysen, with the book,
And I turns the old pages and has a good look
For the text as I've found, as tells me as He
    Were the same trade as me.

Why don't I mark it? Ah, many say so,
But I think I'd as lief, with your leaves, let it go:
It do seem that nice when I fall on it sudden—
    Unexpected, you know!
                CATHERINE C. LIDDELL.

Letty's Globe.

"Letty's Globe" gives us the picture of a little golden-haired girl who covers all Europe with her dainty hands and tresses while giving a kiss to England, her own dear native land. (1808–79.)

WHEN Letty had scarce pass'd her third glad year,
And her young, artless words began to flow,
One day we gave the child a colour'd sphere
Of the wide earth, that she might mark and know,
By tint and outline, all its sea and land.
She patted all the world; old empires peep'd
Between her baby fingers; her soft hand
Was welcome at all frontiers. How she leap'd,
And laugh'd and prattled in her world-wide bliss!
But when we turn'd her sweet unlearned eye
On our own isle, she rais'd a joyous cry,
"Oh! yes, I see it! Letty's home is there!"
And, while she hid all England with a kiss,
Bright over Europe fell her golden hair!
                CHARLES TENNYSON TURNER.

A Dream.

Once a dream did wave a shade
O'er my angel-guarded bed,
That an emmet lost its way
When on grass methought I lay.

Troubled, 'wildered, and forlorn,
Dark, benighted, travel-worn,
Over many a tangled spray,
All heart-broke, I heard her say:

"Oh, my children! do they cry?
Do they hear their father sigh?
Now they look abroad to see,
Now return and weep for me."

Pitying, I dropped a tear;
But I saw a glow-worm near,
Who replied, "What wailing wight
Calls the watchman of the night?

"I am set to light the ground
While the beetle goes his round.
Follow now the beetle's hum—
Little wanderer, hie thee home!"

WILLIAM BLAKE.

Heaven Is Not Reached at a Single Bound.

(A FRAGMENT.)

"We build the ladder by which we climb" is a line worthy of any poet. J. G. Holland (1819–81) has immortalised himself in this line, at least.

HEAVEN is not reached at a single bound,
But we build the ladder by which we rise
From the lowly earth to the vaulted skies,
And we mount to its summit round by round.

I count this thing to be grandly true:
That a noble deed is a step toward God,—
Lifting the soul from the common clod
To a purer air and a broader view.

J. G. HOLLAND.

The Battle of Blenheim.

Have you been to Woodstock, near Oxford, England? If so, you have seen the palace of the Duke of Marlborough, who won the battle of Blenheim. The main point of the poem is the doubtful honour in killing in our great wars. Southey, the poet, lived from 1774 to 1843.

IT was a summer's evening,
Old Kaspar's work was done,
And he before his cottage door
Was sitting in the sun;
And by him sported on the green
His little grandchild Wilhelmine.

She saw her brother Peterkin
Roll something large and round,
Which he, beside the rivulet,
In playing there, had found.

He came to ask what he had found,
That was so large, and smooth, and round.

Old Kaspar took it from the boy,
    Who stood expectant by;
And then the old man shook his head,
    And, with a natural sigh,
"'Tis some poor fellow's skull," said he,
"Who fell in the great victory!

"I find them in the garden,
    For there's many hereabout;
And often when I go to plow,
    The plowshare turns them out;
For many thousand men," said he,
"Were slain in that great victory!"

"Now tell us what 'twas all about,"
    Young Peterkin he cries;
And little Wilhelmine looks up
    With wonder-waiting eyes;
"Now tell us all about the war,
And what they killed each other for."

"It was the English," Kaspar cried,
    "Who put the French to rout;
But what they killed each other for
    I could not well make out.
But everybody said," quoth he,
"That 'twas a famous victory!

"My father lived at Blenheim then,
    Yon little stream hard by:

They burned his dwelling to the ground.
   And he was forced to fly;
So with his wife and child he fled,
Nor had he where to rest his head.

"With fire and sword the country round
   Was wasted far and wide;
And many a childing mother then
   And new-born baby died.
But things like that, you know, must be
At every famous victory.

"They say it was a shocking sight
   After the field was won;
For many thousand bodies here
   Lay rotting in the sun.
But things like that, you know, must be
After a famous victory.

"Great praise the Duke of Marlborough won,
   And our good Prince Eugene."
"Why, 'twas a very wicked thing!"
   Said little Wilhelmine.
"Nay, nay, my little girl," quoth he,
"It was a famous victory!

"And everybody praised the Duke
   Who this great fight did win."
"But what good came of it at last?"
   Quoth little Peterkin.
"Why, that I cannot tell," said he,
"But 'twas a famous victory."

                     ROBERT SOUTHEY.

Fidelity.

"Fidelity," by William Wordsworth (1770–1850), is placed here out of respect to a boy of eleven years who liked the poem well enough to recite it frequently. The scene is laid on Helvellyn, to me the most impressive mountain of the Lake District of England. Wordsworth is a part of this country. I once heard John Burroughs say: "I went to the Lake District to see what kind of a country it could be that would produce a Wordsworth."

A BARKING sound the Shepherd hears,
A cry as of a dog or fox;
He halts—and searches with his eyes
Among the scattered rocks;
And now at distance can discern
A stirring in a brake of fern;
And instantly a Dog is seen,
Glancing through that covert green.

The Dog is not of mountain breed;
Its motions, too, are wild and shy;
With something, as the Shepherd thinks,
Unusual in its cry:
Nor is there any one in sight
All round, in hollow or on height;
Nor shout, nor whistle strikes his ear;
What is the Creature doing here?

It was a cove, a huge recess,
That keeps, till June, December's snow,
A lofty precipice in front,
A silent tarn below!
Far in the bosom of Helvellyn,
Remote from public road or dwelling,
Pathway, or cultivated land;
From trace of human foot or hand.

There sometimes doth a leaping fish
Send through the tarn a lonely cheer;
The crags repeat the raven's croak,
In symphony austere;
Thither the rainbow comes—the cloud—
And mists that spread the flying shroud;
And sunbeams; and the sounding blast,
That, if it could, would hurry past,
But that enormous barrier binds it fast.

Not free from boding thoughts, a while
The Shepherd stood: then makes his way
Toward the Dog, o'er rocks and stones,
As quickly as he may;
Nor far had gone, before he found
A human skeleton on the ground;
The appalled discoverer with a sigh
Looks round, to learn the history.

From those abrupt and perilous rocks
The Man had fallen, that place of fear!
At length upon the Shepherd's mind
It breaks, and all is clear:
He instantly recalled the name,
And who he was, and whence he came;
Remembered, too, the very day
On which the traveller passed this way.

But hear a wonder, for whose sake
This lamentable tale I tell!
A lasting monument of words
This wonder merits well.

The Dog, which still was hovering nigh,
Repeating the same timid cry,
This Dog had been through three months'
    space
A dweller in that savage place.

Yes, proof was plain that, since the day
When this ill-fated traveller died,
The Dog had watched about the spot,
Or by his master's side:
How nourished here through such long
    time
He knows, who gave that love sublime;
And gave that strength of feeling, great
Above all human estimate.

WILLIAM WORDSWORTH.

The Chambered Nautilus.

People are more and more coming to recognise the fact that each individual soul has a right to its own stages of development. "The Chambered Nautilus" is for that reason beloved of the masses. It is one of the grandest poems ever written. "Build thee more stately mansions, O my soul!" This line alone would make the poem immortal. (1809-94.)

THIS is the ship of pearl, which, poets feign,
        Sailed the unshadowed main,—
        The venturous bark that flings
On the sweet summer wind its purpled wings
In gulfs enchanted, where the Siren sings,
        And coral reefs lie bare,
Where the cold sea-maids rise to sun their stream-
    ing hair.

Its webs of living gauze no more unfurl;
     Wrecked is the ship of pearl!
     And every chambered cell,
Where its dim dreaming life was wont to dwell,
As the frail tenant shaped his growing shell,
     Before thee lies revealed,—
Its irised ceiling rent, its sunless crypt unsealed!

Year after year beheld the silent toil
     That spread his lustrous coil;
     Still, as the spiral grew,
He left the past year's dwelling for the new,
Stole with soft step its shining archway through,
     Built up its idle door,
Stretched in his last-found home, and knew the
    old no more.

Thanks for the heavenly message brought by thee,
     Child of the wandering sea,
     Cast from her lap, forlorn!
From thy dead lips a clearer note is born
Than ever Triton blew from wreathèd horn!
     While on mine ear it rings,
Through the deep caves of thought I hear a voice
    that sings:—

Build thee more stately mansions, O my soul,
     As the swift seasons roll!
     Leave thy low-vaulted past!
Let each new temple, nobler than the last,
Shut thee from heaven with a dome more vast,
     Till thou at length art free,
Leaving thine outgrown shell by life's unresting sea!
               OLIVER WENDELL HOLMES.

Crossing the Bar.

Tennyson's (1809–92) "Crossing the Bar" is one of the noblest death-songs ever written. I include it in this volume out of respect to a young Philadelphia publisher who recited it one stormy night before the passengers of a ship when I was crossing the Atlantic, and also because so many young people have the good taste to love it. It has been said that next to Browning's "Prospice" it is the greatest death-song ever written.

SUNSET and evening star,
  And one clear call for me!
And may there be no moaning of the bar,
  When I put out to sea,

But such a tide as moving seems asleep,
  Too full for sound and foam,
When that which drew from out the boundless deep
  Turns again home.

Twilight and evening bell,
  And after that the dark!
And may there be no sadness of farewell,
  When I embark;

For tho' from out our bourne of Time and Place
  The flood may bear me far,
I hope to see my Pilot face to face
  When I have cross'd the bar.

           ALFRED TENNYSON.

The Overland-Mail.

"The Overland-Mail" is a most desirable poem for children to learn. When one boy learns it the others want to follow. It takes as a hero the man who gives common service—the one who does not lead or command, but follows the line of duty. (1865-.)

In the name of the Empress of India, make way,
O Lords of the Jungle wherever you roam,
The woods are astir at the close of the day—
We exiles are waiting for letters from Home—
Let the robber retreat; let the tiger turn tail,
In the name of the Empress the Overland-Mail!

With a jingle of bells as the dusk gathers in,
He turns to the foot-path that leads up the hill—
The bags on his back, and a cloth round his chin,
And, tucked in his belt, the Post-Office bill;—
"Despatched on this date, as received by the rail,
Per runner, two bags of the Overland-Mail."

Is the torrent in spate? He must ford it or swim.
Has the rain wrecked the road? He must climb
    by the cliff.
Does the tempest cry "Halt"? What are tempests
    to him?
The service admits not a "but" or an "if";
While the breath's in his mouth, he must bear
    without fail,
In the name of the Empress the Overland-Mail.

From aloe to rose-oak, from rose-oak to fir,
From level to upland, from upland to crest,

From rice-field to rock-ridge, from rock-ridge to
    spur,
Fly the soft-sandalled feet, strains the brawny
    brown chest.
From rail to ravine—to the peak from the vale—
Up, up through the night goes the Overland-Mail.

There's a speck on the hillside, a dot on the road—
A jingle of bells on the foot-path below—
There's a scuffle above in the monkeys' abode—
The world is awake, and the clouds are aglow—
For the great Sun himself must attend to the
    hail;—
In the name of the Empress the Overland-Mail.

RUDYARD KIPLING.

Gathering Song of Donald Dhu.

Jon, do you remember when you used to spout "Pibroch of Donald
Dhu"? I think you were ten years old. Sir Walter Scott's men all
have a genius for standing up to their guns, and boys gather up the
man's genius when reciting his verse. (1771–1832.)

PIBROCH of Donuil Dhu,
    Pibroch of Donuil,
Wake thy wild voice anew,
    Summon Clan Conuil.
Come away, come away,
    Hark to the summons!
Come in your war-array,
    Gentles and commons.

Come from deep glen, and
    From mountain so rocky,
The war-pipe and pennon
    Are at Inverlochy.

Come every hill-plaid, and
    True heart that wears one,
Come every steel blade, and
    Strong hand that bears one.

Leave untended the herd,
    The flock without shelter;
Leave the corpse uninterr'd,
    The bride at the altar;
Leave the deer, leave the steer,
    Leave nets and barges:
Come with your fighting gear,
    Broadswords and targes.

Come as the winds come, when
    Forests are rended;
Come as the waves come, when
    Navies are stranded:
Faster come, faster come,
    Faster and faster,
Chief, vassal, page, and groom,
    Tenant and master.

Fast they come, fast they come;
    See how they gather!
Wide waves the eagle plume
    Blended with heather,
Cast your plaids, draw your blades,
    Forward each man set!
Pibroch of Donuil Dhu
    Knell for the onset!
              SIR WALTER SCOTT.

Marco Bozzaris.

"Marco Bozzaris," by Fitz-Greene Halleck (1790–1867), was in my old school-reader. Boys and girls liked it then and they like it now. This is another of the poems that was not born to die.

At midnight, in his guarded tent,
  The Turk was dreaming of the hour
When Greece, her knee in suppliance bent,
  Should tremble at his power:
In dreams, through camp and court, he bore
The trophies of a conqueror;
  In dreams his song of triumph heard;
Then wore his monarch's signet ring:
Then pressed that monarch's throne—a king;
As wild his thoughts, and gay of wing,
  As Eden's garden bird.

At midnight, in the forest shades,
  Bozzaris ranged his Suliote band,
True as the steel of their tried blades,
  Heroes in heart and hand.
There had the Persian's thousands stood,
There had the glad earth drunk their blood
  On old Platæa's day;
And now there breathed that haunted air
The sons of sires who conquered there,
With arm to strike and soul to dare,
  As quick, as far as they.

An hour passed on—the Turk awoke;
  That bright dream was his last;
He woke—to hear his sentries shriek,
"To arms! they come! the Greek! the Greek!"

He woke—to die midst flame, and smoke,
And shout, and groan, and sabre-stroke,
  And death-shots falling thick and fast
As lightnings from the mountain-cloud;
And heard, with voice as trumpet loud,
  Bozzaris cheer his band:
"Strike—till the last armed foe expires;
Strike—for your altars and your fires;
Strike—for the green graves of your sires;
  God—and your native land!"

They fought—like brave men, long and well
  They piled that ground with Moslem slain
They conquered—but Bozzaris fell,
  Bleeding at every vein.
His few surviving comrades saw
His smile when rang their proud hurrah,
  And the red field was won;
Then saw in death his eyelids close
Calmly, as to a night's repose,
  Like flowers at set of sun.

Come to the bridal-chamber, Death!
  Come to the mother's, when she feels,
For the first time, her first-born's breath;
  Come when the blessed seals
That close the pestilence are broke,
And crowded cities wail its stroke;
Come in consumption's ghastly form,
The earthquake shock, the ocean storm;
Come when the heart beats high and warm
  With banquet-song, and dance, and win
And thou are terrible—the tear,

The groan, the knell, the pall, the bier,
And all we know, or dream, or fear
  Of agony, are thine.

But to the hero, when his sword
  Has won the battle for the free,
Thy voice sounds like a prophet's word;
And in its hollow tones are heard
  The thanks of millions yet to be.
Come, when his task of fame is wrought—
Come, with her laurel-leaf, blood-bought—
  Come in her crowning hour—and then
Thy sunken eye's unearthly light
To him is welcome as the sight
  Of sky and stars to prisoned men;
Thy grasp is welcome as the hand
Of brother in a foreign land;
Thy summons welcome as the cry
That told the Indian isles were nigh
  To the world-seeking Genoese,
When the land wind, from woods of palm,
And orange-groves, and fields of balm,
  Blew o'er the Haytian seas.

Bozzaris! with the storied brave
  Greece nurtured in her glory's time,
Rest thee—there is no prouder grave,
  Even in her own proud clime.
She wore no funeral-weeds for thee,
  Nor bade the dark hearse wave its plume
Like torn branch from death's leafless tree
In sorrow's pomp and pageantry,
  The heartless luxury of the tomb;

But she remembers thee as one
Long loved and for a season gone;
For thee her poet's lyre is wreathed,
Her marble wrought, her music breathed;
For thee she rings the birthday bells;
Of thee her babe's first lisping tells;
For thine her evening prayer is said
At palace-couch and cottage-bed;
Her soldier, closing with the foe,
Gives for thy sake a deadlier blow;
His plighted maiden, when she fears
For him the joy of her young years,
Thinks of thy fate, and checks her tears;
   And she, the mother of thy boys,
Though in her eye and faded cheek
Is read the grief she will not speak,
   The memory of her buried joys,
And even she who gave thee birth,
Will, by their pilgrim-circled hearth,
   Talk of thy doom without a sigh;
For thou art Freedom's now, and Fame's:
One of the few, the immortal names,
   That were not born to die.

FITZ-GREENE HALLECK.

The Death of Napoleon.

"The Death of Napoleon," by Isaac McClellan (1806–99), was yet
another of the good old reader songs taught us by a teacher of good
taste. We love those teachers more the older we grow.

WILD was the night, yet a wilder night
   Hung round the soldier's pillow;
In his bosom there waged a fiercer fight
   Than the fight on the wrathful billow.

A few fond mourners were kneeling by,
  The few that his stern heart cherished;
They knew, by his glazed and unearthly eye,
  That life had nearly perished.

They knew by his awful and kingly look,
  By the order hastily spoken,
That he dreamed of days when the nations shook,
  And the nations' hosts were broken.

He dreamed that the Frenchman's sword still slew,
  And triumphed the Frenchman's eagle,
And the struggling Austrian fled anew,
  Like the hare before the beagle.

The bearded Russian he scourged again,
  The Prussian's camp was routed,
And again on the hills of haughty Spain
  His mighty armies shouted.

Over Egypt's sands, over Alpine snows,
  At the pyramids, at the mountain,
Where the wave of the lordly Danube flows,
  And by the Italian fountain,

On the snowy cliffs where mountain streams
  Dash by the Switzer's dwelling,
He led again, in his dying dreams,
  His hosts, the proud earth quelling.

Again Marengo's field was won,
  And Jena's bloody battle;
Again the world was overrun,
  Made pale at his cannon's rattle.

He died at the close of that darksome day,
  A day that shall live in story;
In the rocky land they placed his clay,
  "And left him alone with his glory."

ISAAC McCLELLAN.

How Sleep the Brave.

How sleep the brave, who sink to rest
By all their country's wishes blest!
When Spring, with dewy fingers cold,
Returns to deck their hallow'd mould,
She there shall dress a sweeter sod
Than Fancy's feet have ever trod.

By fairy hands their knell is rung,
By forms unseen their dirge is sung:
There Honour comes, a pilgrim gray,
To bless the turf that wraps their clay;
And Freedom shall a while repair
To dwell a weeping hermit there!

WILLIAM COLLINS.

The Flag Goes By.

"The Flag Goes By" is included out of regard to a boy of eleven years who pleased me by his great appreciation of it. It teaches the lesson of reverence to our great national symbol. It is published by permission of the author, Henry Holcomb Bennett, of Ohio. (1863–.)

HATS off!
Along the street there comes
A blare of bugles, a ruffle of drums,
A flash of colour beneath the sky:
        Hats off!
The flag is passing by!

Blue and crimson and white it shines
Over the steel-tipped, ordered lines.
        Hats off!
The colours before us fly;
But more than the flag is passing by.

Sea-fights and land-fights, grim and great,
Fought to make and to save the State:
Weary marches and sinking ships;
Cheers of victory on dying lips;

Days of plenty and years of peace;
March of a strong land's swift increase;
Equal justice, right, and law,
Stately honour and reverend awe;

Sign of a nation, great and strong
Toward her people from foreign wrong:
Pride and glory and honour,—all
Live in the colours to stand or fall.

        Hats off!
Along the street there comes
A blare of bugles; a ruffle of drums;
And loyal hearts are beating high:
        Hats off!
The flag is passing by!
                HENRY HOLCOMB BENNETT.

Hohenlinden.

ON Linden, when the sun was low,
All bloodless lay th' untrodden snow;
And dark as winter was the flow
        Of Iser, rolling rapidly.

But Linden saw another sight,
When the drum beat, at dead of night,
Commanding fires of death to light
 The darkness of her scenery.

By torch and trumpet fast array'd
Each horseman drew his battle-blade,
And furious every charger neigh'd
 To join the dreadful revelry.

Then shook the hills with thunder riven;
Then rush'd the steed to battle driven,
And louder than the bolts of Heaven,
 Far flash'd the red artillery.

But redder yet that light shall glow
On Linden's hills of stainèd snow;
And bloodier yet the torrent flow
 Of Iser, rolling rapidly.

'Tis morn, but scarce yon level sun
Can pierce the war-clouds, rolling dun,
Where furious Frank, and fiery Hun,
 Shout in their sulph'rous canopy.

The combat deepens. On, ye brave
Who rush to glory or the grave!
Wave, Munich! all thy banners wave,
 And charge with all thy chivalry!

Few, few shall part, where many meet!
The snow shall be their winding-sheet,
And every turf beneath their feet
 Shall be a soldier's sepulcher.
     THOMAS CAMPBELL.

My Old Kentucky Home.

THE sun shines bright in the old Kentucky home;
  'Tis summer, the darkeys are gay;
The corn-top's ripe, and the meadow's in the bloom,
  While the birds make music all the day.
The young folks roll on the little cabin floor,
  All merry, all happy and bright;
By-'n'-by hard times comes a-knocking at the
    door:—
  Then my old Kentucky home, good-night!

        Weep no more, my lady,
          O, weep no more to-day!
        We will sing one song for the old Kentucky home,
          For the old Kentucky home, far away.

They hunt no more for the 'possum and the coon,
  On the meadow, the hill, and the shore;
They sing no more by the glimmer of the moon,
  On the bench by the old cabin door.
The day goes by like a shadow o'er the heart,
  With sorrow, where all was delight;
The time has come when the darkeys have to
    part:—
  Then my old Kentucky home, good-night!

The head must bow, and the back will have to bend,
  Wherever the darkey may go;
A few more days, and the trouble all will end,
  In the field where the sugar-canes grow.

A few more days for to tote the weary load,—
  No matter, 'twill never be light;
A few more days till we totter on the road:—
  Then my old Kentucky home, good-night!

    Weep no more, my lady,
    O, weep no more to-day!
  We will sing one song for the old Kentucky home,
    For the old Kentucky home, far away.
           STEPHEN COLLINS FOSTER.

Old Folks at Home.

WAY down upon de Swanee Ribber,
  Far, far away,
Dere's wha my heart is turning ebber,
  Dere's wha de old folks stay.
All up and down de whole creation
  Sadly I roam,
Still longing for de old plantation,
  And for de old folks at home.

    All de world am sad and dreary,
      Eberywhere I roam;
    Oh, darkeys, how my heart grows weary,
      Far from de old folks at home!

All round de little farm I wandered
  When I was young,
Den many happy days I squandered,
  Many de songs I sung.

When I was playing wid my brudder
  Happy was I;
Oh, take me to my kind old mudder!
  Dere let me live and die.

One little hut among de bushes,
  One dat I love,
Still sadly to my memory rushes,
  No matter where I rove.
When will I see de bees a-humming
  All round de comb?
When will I hear de banjo tumming,
  Down in my good old home?

    All de world am sad and dreary,
      Eberywhere I roam;
    Oh, darkeys, how my heart grows weary,
      Far from de old foiks at home!
              STEPHEN COLLINS FOSTER.

The Wreck of the " Hesperus."

"The Wreck of the *Hesperus*," by Longfellow (1807–82), on "Norman's Woe," off the coast near Cape Ann, is a historic poem as well as an imaginative composition.

IT was the schooner *Hesperus*,
  That sailed the wintry sea;
And the skipper had taken his little daughter,
  To bear him company.

Blue were her eyes as the fairy-flax,
  Her cheeks like the dawn of day,
And her bosom white as the hawthorn buds
  That ope in the month of May.

The skipper he stood beside the helm,
  His pipe was in his mouth,
And he watched how the veering flaw did blow
  The smoke now west, now south.

Then up and spake an old sailòr,
  Had sailed the Spanish Main,
"I pray thee put into yonder port,
  For I fear a hurricane.

"Last night the moon had a golden ring,
  And to-night no moon we see!"
The skipper he blew a whiff from his pipe,
  And a scornful laugh laughed he.

Colder and louder blew the wind,
  A gale from the northeast,
The snow fell hissing in the brine,
  And the billows frothed like yeast.

Down came the storm, and smote amain
  The vessel in its strength;
She shuddered and paused, like a frighted steed,
  Then leaped her cable's length.

"Come hither! come hither! my little daughter,
  And do not tremble so;
For I can weather the roughest gale
  That ever wind did blow."

He wrapped her warm in his seaman's coat
  Against the stinging blast;
He cut a rope from a broken spar,
  And bound her to the mast.

"O father! I hear the church-bells ring,
  O say, what may it be?"
"'Tis a fog-bell on a rock-bound coast!"—
  And he steered for the open sea.

"O father! I hear the sound of guns,
  O say, what may it be?"
"Some ship in distress, that cannot live
  In such an angry sea!"

"O father! I see a gleaming light,
  O say, what may it be?"
But the father answered never a word,
  A frozen corpse was he.

Lashed to the helm, all stiff and stark,
  With his face turned to the skies,
The lantern gleamed through the gleaming snow
  On his fixed and glassy eyes.

Then the maiden clasped her hands and prayed
  That savèd she might be;
And she thought of Christ, who stilled the wave
  On the Lake of Galilee.

And fast through the midnight dark and drear,
  Through the whistling sleet and snow,
Like a sheeted ghost the vessel swept
  Toward the reef of Norman's Woe.

And ever the fitful gusts between
  A sound came from the land;
It was the sound of the trampling surf
  On the rocks and the hard sea-sand.

The breakers were right beneath her bows,
 She drifted a dreary wreck,
And a whooping billow swept the crew
 Like icicles from her deck.

She struck where the white and fleecy waves
 Looked soft as carded wool,
But the cruel rocks they gored her side
 Like the horns of an angry bull.

Her rattling shrouds all sheathed in ice,
 With the masts went by the board;
Like a vessel of glass she stove and sank,—
 Ho! ho! the breakers roared!

At daybreak on the bleak sea-beach
 A fisherman stood aghast,
To see the form of a maiden fair
 Lashed close to a drifting mast.

The salt sea was frozen on her breast,
 The salt tears in her eyes;
And he saw her hair, like the brown sea-weed,
 On the billows fall and rise.

Such was the wreck of the *Hesperus*,
 In the midnight and the snow!
Christ save us all from a death like this,
 On the reef of Norman's Woe!

HENRY W. LONGFELLOW.

Bannockburn.

ROBERT BRUCE'S ADDRESS TO HIS ARMY.

You can look down on the battle-field of Bannockburn from Stirling
Castle, Scotland, near which stands a magnificent statue of Robert,
the Bruce. How often have I trodden over the old battle-field!
The monument of William Wallace, too, looms up on the Ochil Hills,
not far away. (1759-96.)

Scots, wha hae wi' Wallace bled,
Scots, wham Bruce has aften led;
Welcome to your gory bed,
　Or to victorie.

Now's the day, and now's the hour;
See the front o' battle lower;
See approach proud Edward's power—
　Chains and slaverie!

Wha will be a traitor knave?
Wha can fill a coward's grave?
Wha sae base as be a slave?
　Let him turn and flee!

Wha for Scotland's King and law
Freedom's sword will strongly draw,
Freeman stand, or freeman fa'?
　Let him follow me!

By oppression's woes and pains!
By your sons in servile chains!
We will drain our dearest veins,
　But they shall be free!

Lay the proud usurpers low!
Tyrants fall in every foe!
Liberty's in every blow!
　Let us do. or die!

　　　　　　　ROBERT BURNS.

PART IV.

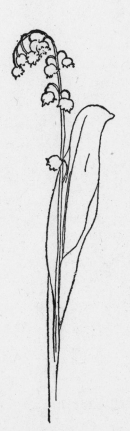

Lad and Lassie

PART IV

The Inchcape Rock.

The man is wrecked and his ship is sunken before he ever steps on board or sees the water if his heart is hard and his estimate of human beings low. "The Inchcape Rock" is a thrust at hard-heartedness. "What is the use of life?" To bear one another's burdens, to develop a genius for pulling people through hard places—that's the use of life. It is the last resort of a mean mind to crack jokes that wreck innocent voyagers on life's sea. (1774-1843.)

No stir in the air, no stir in the sea,
The ship was still as she could be;
Her sails from heaven received no motion;
Her keel was steady in the ocean.

Without either sign or sound of their shock,
The waves flowed over the Inchcape Rock;
So little they rose, so little they fell,
They did not move the Inchcape Bell.

The Abbot of Aberbrothok
Had placed that Bell on the Inchcape Rock;
On a buoy in the storm it floated and swung,
And over the waves its warning rung.

When the Rock was hid by the surge's swell,
The mariners heard the warning Bell;
And then they knew the perilous Rock,
And blest the Abbot of Aberbrothok.

The sun in heaven was shining gay;
All things were joyful on that day;
The sea-birds screamed as they wheeled round,
And there was joyance in their sound.

The buoy of the Inchcape Bell was seen,
A dark spot on the ocean green;
Sir Ralph the Rover walked his deck,
And he fixed his eye on the darker speck.

He felt the cheering power of spring;
It made him whistle, it made him sing:
His heart was mirthful to excess,
But the Rover's mirth was wickedness.

His eye was on the Inchcape float.
Quoth he, "My men, put out the boat
And row me to the Inchcape Rock,
And I'll plague the Abbot of Aberbrothok."

The boat is lowered, the boatmen row,
And to the Inchcape Rock they go;
Sir Ralph bent over from the boat,
And he cut the Bell from the Inchcape float.

Down sank the Bell with a gurgling sound;
The bubbles rose and burst around.
Quoth Sir Ralph, "The next who comes to the
    Rock
Won't bless the Abbot of Aberbrothok."

Sir Ralph the Rover sailed away;
He scoured the sea for many a day;
And now grown rich with plundered store,
He steers his course for Scotland's shore.

So thick a haze o'erspread the sky,
They cannot see the sun on high:

The wind hath blown a gale all day;
At evening it hath died away.

On the deck the Rover takes his stand;
So dark it is they see no land.
Quoth Sir Ralph, "It will be brighter soon,
For there is the dawn of the rising moon."

"Canst hear," said one, "the broken roar?
For methinks we should be near the shore."
"Now where we are I cannot tell,
But I wish I could hear the Inchcape Bell."

They hear no sound; the swell is strong;
Though the wind hath fallen, they drift along
Till the vessel strikes with a shivering shock:
"O Christ! it is the Inchcape Rock!"

Sir Ralph the Rover tore his hair,
He curst himself in his despair:
The waves rush in on every side;
The ship is sinking beneath the tide.

But, even in his dying fear,
One dreadful sound could the Rover hear,—
A sound as if with the Inchcape Bell
The Devil below was ringing his knell.

ROBERT SOUTHEY.

The Finding of the Lyre.

Once a year my pupils teach me "The Finding of the Lyre." By the time I have learned it they know the meaning of every line and have caught the spirit of the verse. There is an ancient "lyre," or violin, made in northern Africa, in the possession of a Boston lady, and I have found the mud-turtle rattle among the Indians on the Indian reservation at Syracuse, New York. They use it as a musical instrument in their Thanksgiving dances. The poem helps to build an interest in history and mythology while it develops a child's reverence and insight. (1819–91.)

THERE lay upon the ocean's shore
What once a tortoise served to cover;
A year and more, with rush and roar,
The surf had rolled it over,
Had played with it, and flung it by,
As wind and weather might decide it,
Then tossed it high where sand-drifts dry
Cheap burial might provide it.

It rested there to bleach or tan,
The rains had soaked, the sun had burned it;
With many a ban the fisherman
Had stumbled o'er and spurned it;
And there the fisher-girl would stay,
Conjecturing with her brother
How in their play the poor estray
Might serve some use or other.

So there it lay, through wet and dry,
As empty as the last new sonnet,
Till by and by came Mercury,
And, having mused upon it,
"Why, here," cried he, "the thing of things
In shape, material, and dimension!
Give it but strings, and, lo, it sings,
A wonderful invention!"

So said, so done; the chords he strained,
And, as his fingers o'er them hovered,
The shell disdained a soul had gained,
The lyre had been discovered.
O empty world that round us lies,
Dead shell, of soul and thought forsaken,
Brought we but eyes like Mercury's,
In thee what songs should waken!

JAMES RUSSELL LOWELL.

A Chrysalis.

"A Chrysalis" is a favourite poem with John Burroughs, and is found, too, in Stedman's collection. We all come to a point in life where we need to burst the shell and fly away into the new realm. (1835-98.)

MY little Mädchen found one day
A curious something in her play,
That was not fruit, nor flower, nor seed;
It was not anything that grew,
Or crept, or climbed, or swam, or flew;
Had neither legs nor wings, indeed;
And yet she was not sure, she said,
Whether it was alive or dead.

She brought it in her tiny hand
To see if I would understand,
And wondered when I made reply,
"You've found a baby butterfly."
"A butterfly is not like this,"
With doubtful look she answered me.
So then I told her what would be
Some day within the chrysalis;

How, slowly, in the dull brown thing
Now still as death, a spotted wing,
And then another, would unfold,
Till from the empty shell would fly
A pretty creature, by and by,
All radiant in blue and gold.

"And will it, truly?" questioned she—
Her laughing lips and eager eyes
All in a sparkle of surprise—
"And shall your little Mädchen see?"
"She shall!" I said.   How could I tell
That ere the worm within its shell
Its gauzy, splendid wings had spread,
My little Mädchen would be dead?

To-day the butterfly has flown,—
She was not here to see it fly,—
And sorrowing I wonder why
The empty shell is mine alone.
Perhaps the secret lies in this:
I too had found a chrysalis,
And Death that robbed me of delight
Was but the radiant creature's flight!

MARY EMILY BRADLEY.

For a' That.

Robert Burns, the plowman and poet, "dinnered wi' a lord." The story goes that he was put at the second table. That lord is dead, but Robert Burns still lives. He is immortal. It is "the survival of the fittest." "For a' That and a' That" is a poem that wipes out the superficial value put on money and other externalities. This poem is more valuable in education than good penmanship or good spelling. (1759-96.)

Is there, for honest poverty,
    That hangs his head, and a' that?
The coward slave, we pass him by,
    We dare be poor for a' that;
For a' that, and a' that,
    Our toils obscure, and a' that;
The rank is but the guinea's stamp,
    The man's the gowd for a' that!

What though on hamely fare we dine,
    Wear hoddin-gray,* and a' that;
Gie fools their silks, and knaves their wine,
    A man's a man for a' that!
For a' that, and a' that,
    Their tinsel show, and a' that;
The honest man, though e'er sae poor,
    Is king o' men for a' that!

Ye see yon birkie † ca'd a lord,
    Wha struts, and stares, and a' that;
Though hundreds worship at his word,
    He's but a coof ‡ for a' that;
For a' that, and a' that,
    His riband, star, and a' that,
The man of independent mind,
    He looks and laughs at a' that.

* Coarse woolen clothes.   † Impudent fellow.   ‡ Fool; blockhead.

A prince can make a belted knight,
    A marquis, duke, and a' that;
But an honest man's aboon his might,
    Guid faith he maunna fa' that!
For a' that, and a' that,
    Their dignities, and a' that,
The pith o' sense, and pride o' worth,
    Are higher rank than a' that.

Then let us pray that come it may—
    As come it will for a' that—
That sense and worth, o'er a' the earth,
    May bear the gree, and a' that;
For a' that, and a' that,
    It's coming yet for a' that,
That man to man, the warld o'er,
    Shall brothers be for a' that!

ROBERT BURNS.

A New Arrival.

"The New Arrival" is a valuable poem because it expresses the joy of a young father over his new baby. If girls should be educated to be good mothers, so should boys be taught that fatherhood is the highest and holiest joy and right of man. The child is educator to the man. He teaches him how to take responsibility, how to give unbiased judgments, and how to be fatherly like "Our Father who is in Heaven." (1844-.)

THERE came to port last Sunday night
    The queerest little craft,
Without an inch of rigging on;
    I looked and looked and laughed.
It seemed so curious that she
    Should cross the Unknown water,
And moor herself right in my room,
    My daughter, O my daughter!

Yet by these presents witness all
    She's welcome fifty times,
And comes consigned to Hope and Love
    And common-meter rhymes.
She has no manifest but this,
    No flag floats o'er the water,
She's too new for the British Lloyds—
    My daughter, O my daughter!

Ring out, wild bells, and tame ones too!
    Ring out the lover's moon!
Ring in the little worsted socks!
    Ring in the bib and spoon!
Ring out the muse! ring in the nurse!
    Ring in the milk and water!
Away with paper, pen, and ink—
    My daughter, O my daughter!
                  GEORGE W. CABLE.

The Brook.

Tennyson's "The Brook" is included out of love to a dear old school-mate in Colorado. The real brook, near Cambridge, England, is tame compared to your Colorado streams, O beloved comrade. This poem is well liked by the majority of pupils. (1809-92.)

I CHATTER, chatter, as I flow
    To join the brimming river;
For men may come and men may go,
    But I go on forever.

I wind about, and in and out,
    With here a blossom sailing,
And here and there a lusty trout,
    And here and there a grayling.

I steal by lawns and grassy plots,
  I slide by hazel covers;
I move the sweet forget-me-nots
  That grow for happy lovers.

I slip, I slide, I gloom, I glance,
  Among my skimming swallows;
I make the netted sunbeams dance
  Against my sandy shallows.

I murmur under moon and stars
  In brambly wildernesses;
I linger by my shingly bars;
  I loiter round my cresses.

And out again I curve and flow
  To join the brimming river;
For men may come and men may go,
  But I go on forever.

ALFRED TENNYSON.

The Ballad of the " Clampherdown."

"The Ballad of the *Clampherdown*," by Rudyard Kipling, is included
because my boys always like it. It needs a great deal of explanation,
and few boys will hold out to the end in learning it. But "it pays."
(1865–.)

IT was our war-ship *Clampherdown*
  Would sweep the Channel clean,
Wherefore she kept her hatches close
When the merry Channel chops arose,
  To save the bleached marine.

She had one bow-gun of a hundred ton,
  And a great stern-gun beside;

They dipped their noses deep in the sea,
They racked their stays and stanchions free
  In the wash of the wind-whipped tide.

It was our war-ship *Clampherdown*,
  Fell in with a cruiser light
That carried the dainty Hotchkiss gun
And a pair o' heels wherewith to run,
  From the grip of a close-fought fight.

She opened fire at seven miles—
  As ye shoot at a bobbing cork—
And once she fired and twice she fired,
Till the bow-gun drooped like a lily tired
  That lolls upon the stalk.

"Captain, the bow-gun melts apace,
  The deck-beams break below,
'Twere well to rest for an hour or twain,
And botch the shattered plates again."
  And he answered, " Make it so."

She opened fire within the mile—
  As ye shoot at the flying duck—
And the great stern-gun shot fair and true,
With the heave of the ship, to the stainless
    blue,
  And the great stern-turret stuck.

"Captain, the turret fills with steam,
  The feed-pipes burst below—
You can hear the hiss of helpless ram,
You can hear the twisted runners jam."
  And he answered, " Turn and go !"

It was our war-ship *Clampherdown*,
   And grimly did she roll;
Swung round to take the cruiser's fire
As the White Whale faces the Thresher's ire,
   When they war by the frozen Pole.

"Captain, the shells are falling fast,
   And faster still fall we;
And it is not meet for English stock,
To bide in the heart of an eight-day clock,
   The death they cannot see."

"Lie down, lie down, my bold A. B.,
   We drift upon her beam;
We dare not ram, for she can run;
And dare ye fire another gun,
   And die in the peeling steam?"

It was our war-ship *Clampherdown*
   That carried an armour-belt;
But fifty feet at stern and bow,
Lay bare as the paunch of the purser's sow,
   To the hail of the Nordenfeldt.

"Captain, they lack us through and through;
   The chilled steel bolts are swift!
We have emptied the bunkers in open sea,
Their shrapnel bursts where our coal should
     be."
   And he answered, "Let her drift."

It was our war-ship *Clampherdown*,
   Swung round upon the tide,

Her two dumb guns glared south and north,
And the blood and the bubbling steam ran
      forth,
    And she ground the cruiser's side.

"Captain, they cry the fight is done,
    They bid you send your sword."
And he answered, "Grapple her stern and bow.
They have asked for the steel. They shall
      have it now;
    Out cutlasses and board!"

It was our war-ship *Clampherdown*,
    Spewed up four hundred men;
And the scalded stokers yelped delight,
As they rolled in the waist and heard the fight,
    Stamp o'er their steel-walled pen.

They cleared the cruiser end to end,
    From conning-tower to hold.
They fought as they fought in Nelson's fleet;
They were stripped to the waist, they were
      bare to the feet,
    As it was in the days of old.

It was the sinking *Clampherdown*
    Heaved up her battered side—
And carried a million pounds in steel,
To the cod and the corpse-fed conger-eel,
    And the scour of the Channel tide.

It was the crew of the *Clampherdown*
    Stood out to sweep the sea,

On a cruiser won from an ancient foe,
As it was in the days of long-ago,
    And as it still shall be.

                    RUDYARD KIPLING.

The Destruction of Sennacherib.

"The Destruction of Sennacherib," by Lord Byron, finds a place in this collection because Johnnie, a ten-year-old, and many of his friends say, "It's great." (1788-1824.)

THE Assyrian came down like a wolf on the fold,
And his cohorts were gleaming in purple and gold;
And the sheen of their spears was like stars on the
    sea,
When the blue wave rolls nightly on deep Galilee.

Like the leaves of the forest when the Summer is
    green,
That host with their banners at sunset were seen:
Like the leaves of the forest when Autumn hath
    blown,
That host on the morrow lay withered and strown.

For the Angel of Death spread his wings on the
    blast,
And breathed in the face of the foe as he passed;
And the eyes of the sleepers waxed deadly and chill,
And their hearts but once heaved, and forever
    grew still!

And there lay the steed with his nostril all wide,
But through it there rolled not the breath of his
    pride;

And the foam of his gasping lay white on the turf,
And cold as the spray of the rock-beating surf.

And there lay the rider distorted and pale,
With the dew on his brow, and the rust on his mail,
And the tents were all silent, the banners alone,
The lances unlifted, the trumpet unblown.

And the widows of Ashur are loud in their wail,
And the idols are broke in the temple of Baal;
And the might of the Gentile, unsmote by the sword,
Hath melted like snow in the glance of the Lord!

LORD BYRON.

I Remember, I Remember.

I REMEMBER, I remember
The house where I was born,
The little window where the sun
Came peeping in at morn;
He never came a wink too soon
Nor brought too long a day;
But now, I often wish the night
Had borne my breath away.

I remember, I remember
The roses, red and white,
The violets, and the lily-cups—
Those flowers made of light!
The lilacs where the robin built,
And where my brother set
The laburnum on his birthday,—
The tree is living yet!

I remember, I remember
Where I was used to swing,
And thought the air must rush as fresh
To swallows on the wing;
My spirit flew in feathers then
That is so heavy now,
And summer pools could hardly cool
The fever on my brow.

I remember, I remember
The fir trees dark and high;
I used to think their slender tops
Were close against the sky:
It was a childish ignorance,
But now 'tis little joy
To know I'm farther off from Heaven
Than when I was a boy.

THOMAS HOOD.

Driving Home the Cows.

OUT of the clover and blue-eyed grass
   He turned them into the river lane;
One after another he let them pass,
   Then fastened the meadow bars again.

Under the willows and over the hill,
   He patiently followed their sober pace;
The merry whistle for once was still,
   And something shadowed the sunny face.

Only a boy! and his father had said
   He never could let his youngest go:
Two already were lying dead,
   Under the feet of the trampling foe.

But after the evening work was done,
    And the frogs were loud in the meadow-swamp,
Over his shoulder he slung his gun,
    And stealthily followed the footpath damp.

Across the clover, and through the wheat,
    With resolute heart and purpose grim:
Though the dew was on his hurrying feet,
    And the blind bat's flitting startled him.

Thrice since then had the lanes been white,
    And the orchards sweet with apple-bloom;
And now, when the cows came back at night,
    The feeble father drove them home.

For news had come to the lonely farm
    That three were lying where two had lain;
And the old man's tremulous, palsied arm
    Could never lean on a son's again.

The summer day grew cool and late:
    He went for the cows when the work was done;
But down the lane, as he opened the gate,
    He saw them coming one by one:

Brindle, Ebony, Speckle, and Bess,
    Shaking their horns in the evening wind;
Cropping the buttercups out of the grass,
    But who was it following close behind?

Loosely swung in the idle air
    The empty sleeve of army blue;
And worn and pale, from the crisping hair,
    Looked out a face that the father knew.

For close-barred prisons will sometimes yawn,
    And yield their dead unto life again;
And the day that comes with a cloudy dawn,
    In golden glory at last may wane.

The great tears sprang to their meeting eyes;
    For the heart must speak when the lips are dumb,
And under the silent evening skies
    Together they followed the cattle home.

                       KATE PUTNAM OSGOOD.

Krinken.

"Krinken" is the dearest of poems.
      "Krinken was a little child.
        It was summer when he smiled!"
Eugene Field, above all other poets, paid the finest tribute to
children. This poet only, could make the whole ocean warm because
a child's heart was there to warm it.

    KRINKEN was a little child,—
    It was summer when he smiled.
    Oft the hoary sea and grim
    Stretched its white arms out to him,
    Calling, "Sun-child, come to me;
    Let me warm my heart with thee!"
    But the child heard not the sea
    Calling, yearning evermore
    For the summer on the shore.

    Krinken on the beach one day
    Saw a maiden Nis at play;
    On the pebbly beach she played
    In the summer Krinken made.
    Fair, and very fair, was she,
    Just a little child was he.

"Krinken," said the maiden Nis,
"Let me have a little kiss,—
Just a kiss, and go with me
To the summer-lands that be
Down within the silver sea."

Krinken was a little child—
By the maiden Nis beguiled,
Hand in hand with her went he
And 'twas summer in the sea.
And the hoary sea and grim
To its bosom folded him—
Clasped and kissed the little form,
And the ocean's heart was warm.

Now the sea calls out no more;
It is winter on the shore,—
Winter where that little child
Made sweet summer when he smiled;
Though 'tis summer on the sea
Where with maiden Nis went he,—
It is winter on the shore,
Winter, winter evermore.

Of the summer on the deep
Come sweet visions in my sleep:
His fair face lifts from the sea,
His dear voice calls out to me,—
These my dreams of summer be.

Krinken was a little child,
By the maiden Nis beguiled;
Oft the hoary sea and grim
Reached its longing arms to him,

Crying, "Sun-child, come to me;
Let me warm my heart with thee!"
But the sea calls out no more;
It is winter on the shore,—
Winter, cold and dark and wild.

Krinken was a little child,—
It was summer when he smiled;
Down he went into the sea,
And the winter bides with me,
Just a little child was he.

EUGENE FIELD.

Stevenson's Birthday.

"How I should like a birthday!" said the child,
  "I have so few, and they so far apart."
She spoke to Stevenson—the Master smiled—
  "Mine is to-day; I would with all my heart
That it were yours; too many years have I!
Too swift they come, and all too swiftly fly."

So by a formal deed he there conveyed
  All right and title in his natal day,
  To have and hold, to sell or give away,—
Then signed, and gave it to the little maid.

Joyful, yet fearing to believe too much,
  She took the deed, but scarcely dared unfold.
Ah, liberal Genius! at whose potent touch
  All common things shine with transmuted gold!
A day of Stevenson's will prove to be
Not part of Time, but Immortality.

KATHERINE MILLER.

A Modest Wit.

I learned "A Modest Wit" as a reading-lesson when I was a child. It has clung to me and so I cling to it. It is just as good as it ever was. It is a sharp thrust at power that depends on externalities. Selleck Osborne. (————.)

A SUPERCILIOUS nabob of the East—
  Haughty, being great—purse-proud, being rich—
A governor, or general, at the least,
  I have forgotten which—
Had in his family a humble youth,
  Who went from England in his patron's suit,
An unassuming boy, in truth
  A lad of decent parts, and good repute.

This youth had sense and spirit;
  But yet with all his sense,
  Excessive diffidence
Obscured his merit.

One day, at table, flushed with pride and wine,
  His honour, proudly free, severely merry,
Conceived it would be vastly fine
  To crack a joke upon his secretary.

"Young man," he said, "by what art, craft, or
      trade,
  Did your good father gain a livelihood?"—
"He was a saddler, sir," Modestus said,
  "And in his time was reckon'd good."

"A saddler, eh! and taught you Greek,
  Instead of teaching you to sew!
Pray, why did not your father make
  A saddler, sir, of you?"

Each parasite, then, as in duty bound,
The joke applauded, and the laugh went round.
  At length Modestus, bowing low,
Said (craving pardon, if too free he made),
  "Sir, by your leave, I fain would know
Your father's trade!"

"My father's trade! by heaven, that's too bad!
My father's trade? Why, blockhead, are you
    mad?
My father, sir, did never stoop so low—
He was a gentleman, I'd have you know."

"Excuse the liberty I take,"
  Modestus said, with archness on his brow,
"Pray, why did not your father make
  A gentleman of you?"

                        SELLECK OSBORNE.

The Legend of Bishop Hatto.

"The Legend of Bishop Hatto" is doubtless a myth (Robert Southey, 1774–1843). But "The Mouse-Tower on the Rhine" is an object of interest to travellers, and the story has a point.

THE summer and autumn had been so wet,
That in winter the corn was growing yet:
'Twas a piteous sight to see, all around,
The grain lie rotting on the ground.

Every day the starving poor
Crowded around Bishop Hatto's door;
For he had a plentiful last-year's store,
And all the neighbourhood could tell
His granaries were furnished well.

At last Bishop Hatto appointed a day
To quiet the poor without delay:
He bade them to his great barn repair,
And they should have food for winter there.

Rejoiced such tidings good to hear,
The poor folk flocked from far and near;
The great barn was full as it could hold
Of women and children, and young and old.

Then, when he saw it could hold no more,
Bishop Hatto, he made fast the door;
And while for mercy on Christ they call,
He set fire to the barn and burned them all.

"I' faith, 'tis an excellent bonfire!" quoth he;
"And the country is greatly obliged to me
For ridding it in these times forlorn
Of Rats that only consume the corn."

So then to his palace returnèd he,
And he sat down to supper merrily,
And he slept that night like an innocent man;
But Bishop Hatto never slept again.

In the morning as he entered the hall,
Where his picture hung against the wall,
A sweat-like death all over him came;
For the Rats had eaten it out of the frame.

As he looked, there came a man from his farm;
He had a countenance white with alarm:
"My Lord, I opened your granaries this morn,
And the Rats had eaten all your corn."

Another came running presently,
And he was pale as pale could be:
"Fly, my Lord Bishop, fly!" quoth he,
"Ten thousand Rats are coming this way;
The Lord forgive you yesterday!"

"I'll go to my town on the Rhine," replied he;
"'Tis the safest place in Germany;
The walls are high, and the shores are steep,
And the stream is strong, and the water deep."

Bishop Hatto fearfully hastened away,
And he crossed the Rhine without delay,
And reached his tower, and barred with care
All windows, doors, and loop-holes there.

He laid him down, and closed his eyes;
But soon a scream made him arise:
He started and saw two eyes of flame
On his pillow, from whence the screaming came.

He listened and looked; it was only the cat:
But the Bishop he grew more fearful for that;
For she sat screaming, mad with fear
At the army of Rats that was drawing near.

For they have swum over the river so deep,
And they have climbed the shore so steep;
And up the tower their way is bent,
To do the work for which they were sent.

They are not to be told by the dozen or score;
By thousands they come, and by myriads and
    more;

Such numbers had never been heard of before,
Such a judgment had never been witnessed of
  yore.

Down on his knees the Bishop fell,
And faster and faster his beads did tell,
As, louder and louder drawing near,
The gnawing of their teeth he could hear.

And in at the windows and in at the door,
And through the walls, helter-skelter they pour,
And down from the ceiling and up through the
  floor,
From the right and the left, from behind and
  before,
And all at once to the Bishop they go.

They have whetted their teeth against the
  stones;
And now they pick the Bishop's bones:
They gnawed the flesh from every limb;
For they were sent to do judgment on him!

ROBERT SOUTHEY.

Columbus.

We are greatly indebted to Joaquin Miller for his "Sail On! Sail On!"
Endurance is the watchword of the poem and the watchword of our
republic. Every man to his gun! Columbus discovered America in
his own mind before he realised it or proved its existence. I have
often drawn a chart of Columbus's life and voyages to show what need
he had of the motto "Sail On!" to accomplish his end. This is one
of our greatest American poems. The writer still lives in California.

BEHIND him lay the gray Azores,
  Behind the gates of Hercules;
Before him not the ghost of shores,
  Before him only shoreless seas.

The good mate said: "Now must we pray,
　For lo! the very stars are gone;
Speak, Admiral, what shall I say?"
　"Why say, sail on! and on!"

"My men grow mut'nous day by day;
　My men grow ghastly wan and weak."
The stout mate thought of home; a spray
　Of salt wave wash'd his swarthy cheek.
"What shall I say, brave Admiral,
　If we sight naught but seas at dawn?"
"Why, you shall say, at break of day:
　'Sail on! sail on! and on!'"

They sailed and sailed, as winds might blow,
　Until at last the blanch'd mate said;
"Why, now, not even God would know
　Should I and all my men fall dead.
These very winds forget their way,
　For God from these dread seas is gone.
Now speak, brave Admiral, and say——"
　He said: "Sail on! and on!"

They sailed, they sailed, then spoke his mate:
　"This mad sea shows his teeth to-night,
He curls his lip, he lies in wait,
　With lifted teeth as if to bite!
Brave Admiral, say but one word;
　What shall we do when hope is gone?"
The words leaped as a leaping sword:
　"Sail on! sail on! and on!"

Then, pale and worn, he kept his deck,
　And thro' the darkness peered that night.

Ah, darkest night! and then a speck—
    A light! a light! a light! a light!
It grew—a star-lit flag unfurled!
    It grew to be Time's burst of dawn;
He gained a world! he gave that world
    Its watch-word: "On! and on!"
                    JOAQUIN MILLER.

The Shepherd of King Admetus.

Once a year the children learn "The Shepherd of King Admetus," which is one of the finest poems ever written as showing the possible growth of real history into mythology, the tendency of mankind to deify what is fine or sublime in human action. Not every child will learn this entire poem, because it is so long. But every child will learn the best lines in it while the children are teaching it to me and when I take my turn in teaching it to them. No child fails to catch the spirit and intent of the poem and to become entirely familiar with it. (1819–91.)

THERE came a youth upon the earth,
    Some thousand years ago,
Whose slender hands were nothing worth,
    Whether to plow, or reap, or sow.

Upon an empty tortoise-shell
    He stretched some chords, and drew
Music that made men's bosoms swell
    Fearless, or brimmed their eyes with dew.

Then King Admetus, one who had
    Pure taste by right divine,
Decreed his singing not too bad
    To hear between the cups of wine:

And so, well pleased with being soothed
    Into a sweet half-sleep,

Three times his kingly beard he smoothed,
    And made him viceroy o'er his sheep.

His words were simple words enough,
    And yet he used them so,
That what in other mouths was rough
    In his seemed musical and low.

Men called him but a shiftless youth,
    In whom no good they saw;
And yet, unwittingly, in truth,
    They made his careless words their law.

They knew not how he learned at all,
    For idly, hour by hour,
He sat and watched the dead leaves fall,
    Or mused upon a common flower.

It seemed the loveliness of things
    Did teach him all their use,
For, in mere weeds, and stones, and springs,
    He found a healing power profuse.

Men granted that his speech was wise.
    But, when a glance they caught
Of his slim grace and woman's eyes,
    They laughed, and called him good-for-
        naught.

Yet after he was dead and gone,
    And e'en his memory dim,
Earth seemed more sweet to live upon,
    More full of love, because of him.

And day by day more holy grew
　　Each spot where he had trod,
Till after-poets only knew
　　Their first-born brother as a god.
JAMES RUSSELL LOWELL.

How They Brought the Good News from Ghent to Aix.

I have an old essay written by a lad of fourteen years on "How They Brought the Good News from Ghent to Aix." I should judge from this essay that any boy at that age would like the poem, even if he had not himself been over the ground as this boy had. (1812-89.)

I SPRANG to the stirrup, and Joris, and he;
I galloped, Dirck galloped, we galloped all three;
"Good speed!" cried the watch as the gate-bolts
　　undrew;
"Speed!" echoed the wall to us galloping through;
Behind shut the postern, the lights sank to rest,
And into the midnight we galloped abreast.

Not a word to each other; we kept the great pace
Neck by neck, stride by stride, never changing our
　　place;
I turned in my saddle and made its girth tight,
Then shortened each stirrup, and set the pique
　　right,
Rebuckled the cheek-strap, chained slacker the
　　bit,
Nor galloped less steadily Roland a whit.

'Twas moonset at starting; but while we drew near
Lokeren, the cocks crew and twilight dawned
　　clear;

At Boom, a great yellow star came out to see;
At Düffeld, 'twas morning as plain as could be;
And from Mecheln church-steeple we heard the
    half-chime,
So Joris broke silence with, "Yet there is time!"

At Aershot, up leaped of a sudden the sun,
And against him the cattle stood black every one,
To stare through the mist at us galloping past,
And I saw my stout galloper Roland at last,
With resolute shoulders, each butting away
The haze, as some bluff river headland its spray:

And his low head and crest, just one sharp ear
    bent back
For my voice, and the other pricked out on his
    track;
And one eye's black intelligence,—ever that glance
O'er its white edge at me, his own master, askance!
And the thick, heavy spume-flakes which aye
    and anon
His fierce lips shook upward in galloping on.

By Hasselt, Dirck groaned; and cried Joris, "Stay
    spur!
Your Roos galloped bravely, the fault's not in her,
We'll remember at Aix"—for one heard the quick
    wheeze
Of her chest, saw the stretched neck and staggering
    knees,
And sunk tail, and horrible heave of the flank,
As down on her haunches she shuddered and sank.

So, we were left galloping, Joris and I,
Past Looz and past Tongres, no cloud in the sky;
The broad sun above laughed a pitiless laugh,
'Neath our feet broke the brittle bright stubble
like chaff;
Till over by Dalhem a dome-spire sprang white,
And "Gallop," gasped Joris, "for Aix is in sight!"

"How they'll greet us!"—and all in a moment
his roan
Rolled neck and croup over, lay dead as a stone;
And there was my Roland to bear the whole
weight
Of the news which alone could save Aix from her
fate,
With his nostrils like pits full of blood to the brim,
And with circles of red for his eye-sockets' rim.

Then I cast loose my buff-coat, each holster let fall,
Shook off both my jack-boots, let go belt and all,
Stood up in the stirrup, leaned, patted his ear,
Called my Roland his pet-name, my horse without
peer;
Clapped my hands, laughed and sang, any noise,
bad or good,
Till at length into Aix Roland galloped and stood.

And all I remember is—friends flocking round
As I sat with his head 'twixt my knees on the
ground;
And no voice but was praising this Roland of
mine,
As I poured down his throat our last measure of
wine,

Which (the burgesses voted by common consent)
Was no more than his due who brought good news
   from Ghent.

ROBERT BROWNING.

The Burial of Sir John Moore at Corunna.

"The Burial of Sir John Moore" was one of my reading-lessons when I was a child. A distinguished teacher says: "It has become a part of popular education, as has also "The Eve of Waterloo" and "The Death of Napoleon." They are all poems of great rhythmical swing, intense and graphic. (1791-1823.)

NOT a drum was heard, not a funeral note,
   As his corse to the rampart we hurried;
Not a soldier discharged his farewell shot
   O'er the grave where our hero we buried.

We buried him darkly at dead of night,
   The sods with our bayonets turning;
By the struggling moonbeam's misty light,
   And the lantern dimly burning.

No useless coffin enclosed his breast,
   Not in sheet nor in shroud we wound him;
But he lay like a warrior taking his rest,
   With his martial cloak around him.

Few and short were the prayers we said,
   And we spoke not a word of sorrow;
But we steadfastly gazed on the face that was dead,
   And we bitterly thought of the morrow.

We thought, as we hollow'd his narrow bed,
   And smoothed down his lonely pillow,

That the foe and the stranger would tread o'er his
    head,
  And we far away on the billow!

Lightly they'll talk of the spirit that's gone,
  And o'er his cold ashes upbraid him,—
But little he'll reck, if they let him sleep on
  In the grave where a Briton has laid him.

But half of our heavy task was done
  When the clock struck the hour for retiring;
And we heard the distant and random gun
  That the foe was sullenly firing.

Slowly and sadly we laid him down,
  From the field of his fame fresh and gory;
We carved not a line, and we raised not a stone—
  But we left him alone with his glory!

C. Wolfe.

The Eve of Waterloo.

"The Eve of Waterloo," by Lord Byron (1788-1824). Here is another
old reading-book gem that will always be dear to every boy's heart if
he only reads it a few times.

There was a sound of revelry by night,
  And Belgium's capital had gathered then
Her beauty and her chivalry, and bright
  The lamps shone o'er fair women and brave men.
A thousand hearts beat happily; and when
  Music arose with its voluptuous swell,
Soft eyes looked love to eyes which spake again,
  And all went merry as a marriage-bell:
    But hush! hark! a deep sound strikes like a
      rising knell!

Did ye not hear it?   No; 'twas but the wind,
  Or the car rattling o'er the stony street.
On with the dance! let joy be unconfined!
  No sleep till morn, when Youth and Pleasure
    meet
To chase the glowing hours with flying feet!
  But hark!—that heavy sound breaks in once
    more,
As if the clouds its echo would repeat;
  And nearer, clearer, deadlier, than before!
  Arm! arm! it is—it is the cannon's opening roar!

Ah! then and there was hurrying to and fro,
  And gathering tears, and tremblings of distress
And cheeks all pale, which, but an hour ago,
  Blushed at the praise of their own loveliness;
And there were sudden partings, such as press
  The life from out young hearts, and choking sighs
Which ne'er might be repeated: who could guess
  If ever more should meet those mutual eyes,
  Since upon night so sweet such awful morn
    could rise?

And there was mounting in hot haste: the steed,
  The mustering squadron, and the clattering car
Went pouring forward with impetuous speed,
  And swiftly forming in the ranks of war;
And the deep thunder peal on peal afar;
  And near, the beat of the alarming drum
Roused up the soldier ere the morning star;
  While thronged the citizens with terror dumb,
  Or whispering with white lips, "The foe!   They
    come!   They come!"

And Ardennes waves above them her green leaves,
    Dewy with Nature's tear-drops, as they pass,
Grieving, if aught inanimate e'er grieves,
    Over the unreturning brave—alas!
Ere evening to be trodden like the grass
    Which, now beneath them, but above shall grow
In its next verdure, when this fiery mass
    Of living valour, rolling on the foe,
    And burning with high hope, shall moulder cold
        and low.

Last noon beheld them full of lusty life,
    Last eve in Beauty's circle proudly gay;
The midnight brought the signal-sound of strife,
    The morn the marshalling in arms,—the day,
Battle's magnificently stern array!
    The thunder-clouds close o'er it, which, when
        rent,
The earth is covered thick with other clay,
    Which her own clay shall cover, heaped and pent,
    Rider, and horse—friend, foe—in one red burial
        blent!

LORD BYRON.

Ivry.

A SONG OF THE HUGUENOTS.

Laddie, aged eleven, do you remember how you studied and recited "King Henry of Navarre" every poetry hour for a year? It was a long poem, but you stuck to it to the end. We did not know the meaning of a certain word, but I found it up in Switzerland. It is the name of a little town. (1800–59.)

Now glory to the Lord of Hosts, from whom all
    glories are!
And glory to our Sovereign Liege, King Henry of
    Navarre!

Now let there be the merry sound of music and of
    dance,
Through thy corn-fields green, and sunny vines, O
    pleasant land of France!
And thou, Rochelle, our own Rochelle, proud city
    of the waters,
Again let rapture light the eyes of all thy mourning
    daughters.
As thou wert constant in our ills, be joyous in our
    joy,
For cold, and stiff, and still are they who wrought
    thy walls annoy.
Hurrah! Hurrah! a single field hath turned the
    chance of war,
Hurrah! Hurrah! for Ivry, and Henry of Navarre.

Oh! how our hearts were beating, when, at the
    dawn of day,
We saw the army of the League drawn out in long
    array;
With all its priest-led citizens, and all its rebel
    peers,
And Appenzel's stout infantry, and Egmont's
    Flemish spears.
There rode the brood of false Lorraine, the curses
    of our land;
And dark Mayenne was in the midst, a truncheon
    in his hand;
And, as we looked on them, we thought of Seine's
    empurpled flood,
And good Coligni's hoary hair all dabbled with his
    blood;

And we cried unto the living God, who rules the
fate of war,
To fight for His own holy name, and Henry of
Navarre.

The King is come to marshal us, in all his armour
drest,
And he has bound a snow-white plume upon his
gallant crest.
He looked upon his people, and a tear was in his
eye;
He looked upon the traitors, and his glance was
stern and high.
Right graciously he smiled on us, as rolled from
wing to wing,
Down all our line, a deafening shout, "God save
our Lord the King!"
"And if my standard-bearer fall, as fall full well
he may,
For never saw I promise yet of such a bloody fray,
Press where ye see my white plume shine, amid
the ranks of war,
And be your oriflamme to-day the helmet of
Navarre."

Hurrah! the foes are moving. Hark to the
mingled din
Of fife, and steed, and trump, and drum, and
roaring culverin.
The fiery Duke is pricking fast across St. André's
plain,
With all the hireling chivalry of Guelders and
Almayne.

Now by the lips of those ye love, fair gentlemen
    of France,
Charge for the golden lilies,—upon them with the
    lance.
A thousand spurs are striking deep, a thousand
    spears in rest,
A thousand knights are pressing close behind the
    snow-white crest;
And in they burst, and on they rushed, while like
    a guiding star,
Amid the thickest carnage blazed the helmet of
    Navarre.

Now, God be praised, the day is ours. Mayenne
    hath turned his rein.
D'Aumale hath cried for quarter. The Flemish
    count is slain.
Their ranks are breaking like thin clouds before a
    Biscay gale;
The field is heaped with bleeding steeds, and flags,
    and cloven mail.
And then we thought on vengeance, and, all along
    our van,
"Remember St. Bartholomew!" was passed from
    man to man.
But out spake gentle Henry, "No Frenchman is
    my foe:
Down, down with every foreigner, but let your
    brethren go."
Oh! was there ever such a knight, in friendship or
    in war,
As our Sovereign Lord, King Henry, the soldier of
    Navarre?

Right well fought all the Frenchmen who fought
    for France to-day;
And many a lordly banner God gave them for a
    prey.
But we of the Religion have borne us best in fight;
And the good lord of Rosny has ta'en the cornet
    white.
Our own true Maximilian the cornet white hath ta'en,
The cornet white with crosses black, the flag of
    false Lorraine.
Up with it high; unfurl it wide; that all the host
    may know
How God hath humbled the proud house which
    wrought His church such woe.
Then on the ground, while trumpets sound their
    loudest points of war,
Fling the red shreds, a footcloth meet for Henry of
    Navarre.

Ho! maidens of Vienna; Ho! matrons of Lucerne;
Weep, weep, and rend your hair for those who
    never shall return.
Ho! Philip, send, for charity, thy Mexican pistoles,
That Antwerp monks may sing a mass for thy poor
    spearmen's souls.
Ho! gallant nobles of the League, look that your
    arms be bright;
Ho! burghers of Saint Genevieve, keep watch and
    ward to-night.
For our God hath crushed the tyrant, our God
    hath raised the slave,
And mocked the counsel of the wise, the valour of
    the brave.

Then glory to His holy name, from whom all
 glories are;
And glory to our Sovereign Lord, King Henry of
 Navarre.

THOMAS B. MACAULAY.

The Glove and the Lions.

"The Glove and the Lions" was one of my early reading-lessons.
It is an incisive thrust at the vanity of "fair" women. A woman
should be a "true knight" as well as a man. Leigh Hunt (1784–1859).

KING FRANCIS was a hearty king, and loved a
 royal sport,
And one day as his lions fought, sat looking on
 the court;
The nobles filled the benches, with the ladies in
 their pride,
And 'mong them sat the Count de Lorge with
 one for whom he sighed:
And truly 'twas a gallant thing to see that crowning
 show,
Valour, and love, and a king above, and the
 royal beasts below.

Ramp'd and roar'd the lions, with horrid laughing
 jaws;
They bit, they glared, gave blows like beams, a
 wind went with their paws;
With wallowing might and stifled roar they
 rolled on one another,
Till all the pit with sand and mane was in a
 thunderous smother;

The bloody foam above the bars came whisking
  through the air;
Said Francis then, "Faith, gentlemen, we're better
  here than there."

De Lorge's love o'erheard the King,—a beauteous
  lively dame
With smiling lips and sharp, bright eyes, which
  always seem'd the same:
She thought, "The Count, my lover, is brave as
  brave can be;
He surely would do wondrous things to show his
  love of me;
King, ladies, lovers, all look on; the occasion is
  divine;
I'll drop my glove, to prove his love; great glory
  will be mine."

She dropp'd her glove, to prove his love, then
  look'd at him and smiled;
He bowed, and in a moment leapt among the
  lions wild:
His leap was quick, return was quick, he has
  regain'd his place,
Then threw the glove, but not with love, right in
  the lady's face.
"Well done!" cried Francis, "bravely done!"
  and he rose from where he sat:
"No love," quoth he, "but vanity, sets love a
  task like that."

LEIGH HUNT.

The Well of St. Keyne.

I found the Well of St. Keyne in Cornwall, England—not the
poem, but the real well.   The poem is of the great body of world-lore.
Southey (1774-1843).

A WELL there is in the west country,
    And a clearer one never was seen;
There is not a wife in the west-country
    But has heard of the Well of St. Keyne.

An oak and an elm tree stand beside,
    And behind does an ash tree grow,
And a willow from the bank above
    Droops to the water below.

A traveller came to the Well of St. Keyne:
    Pleasant it was to his eye,
For from cock-crow he had been travelling
    And there was not a cloud in the sky.

He drank of the water so cool and clear,
    For thirsty and hot was he,
And he sat down upon the bank,
    Under the willow tree.

There came a man from the neighbouring town
    At the well to fill his pail;
On the well-side he rested it,
    And bade the stranger hail.

"Now, art thou a bachelor, stranger?" quoth he,
    "For an if thou hast a wife,
The happiest draught thou hast drunk this day
    That ever thou didst in thy life.

"Or has your good woman, if one you have,
  In Cornwall ever been?
For an if she have, I'll venture my life
  She has drunk of the Well of St. Keyne."

"I have left a good woman who never was
    here,"
  The stranger he made reply;
"But that my draught should be better for
    that,
  I pray you answer me why."

"St. Keyne," quoth the countryman, "many
    a time
  Drank of this crystal well,
And before the angel summoned her
  She laid on the water a spell.

"If the husband of this gifted well
  Shall drink before his wife,
A happy man thenceforth is he,
  For he shall be master for life.

"But if the wife should drink of it first,
  God help the husband then!"
The stranger stoop'd to the Well of St. Keyne,
  And drank of the waters again.

"You drank of the well, I warrant, betimes?"
  He to the countryman said;
But the countryman smiled as the stranger
    spake,
  And sheepishly shook his head.

"I hastened as soon as the wedding was done,
    And left my wife in the porch,
But i' faith she had been wiser than me,
    For she took a bottle to church."

ROBERT SOUTHEY.

The Nautilus and the Ammonite.

"The Nautilus and the Ammonite" finds a place here out of respect to a twelve-year-old girl who recited it at one of our poetry hours years ago. It made a profound impression on the fifty pupils assembled. I never read it without feeling that it stands test.   Anonymous.

THE nautilus and the ammonite
    Were launched in friendly strife,
Each sent to float in its tiny boat
    On the wide, wide sea of life.

For each could swim on the ocean's brim,
    And, when wearied, its sail could furl,
And sink to sleep in the great sea-deep,
    It its palace all of pearl.

And theirs was a bliss more fair than this
    Which we taste in our colder clime;
For they were rife in a tropic life—
    A brighter and better clime.

They swam 'mid isles whose summer smiles
    Were dimmed by no alloy;
Whose groves were palm, whose air was balm,
    And life one only joy.

They sailed all day through creek and bay,
    And traversed the ocean deep;

And at night they sank on a coral bank,
    In its fairy bowers to sleep.

And the monsters vast of ages past
    They beheld in their ocean caves;
They saw them ride in their power and pride,
    And sink in their deep-sea graves.

And hand in hand, from strand to strand,
    They sailed in mirth and glee;
These fairy shells, with their crystal cells,
    Twin sisters of the sea.

And they came at last to a sea long past,
    But as they reached its shore,
The Almighty's breath spoke out in death,
    And the ammonite was no more.

So the nautilus now in its shelly prow,
    As over the deep it strays,
Still seems to seek, in bay and creek,
    Its companion of other days.

And alike do we, on life's stormy sea,
    As we roam from shore to shore,
Thus tempest-tossed, seek the loved, the lost,
    And find them on earth no more.

Yet the hope how sweet, again to meet,
    As we look to a distant strand,
Where heart meets heart, and no more they part
    Who meet in that better land.

                              ANONYMOUS.

The Solitude of Alexander Selkirk.

I AM monarch of all I survey,
 My right there is none to dispute,
From the center all round to the sea,
 I am lord of the fowl and the brute.
O Solitude! where are the charms
 That sages have seen in thy face?
Better dwell in the midst of alarms
 Than reign in this horrible place.

I am out of humanity's reach,
 I must finish my journey alone,
Never hear the sweet music of speech,—
 I start at the sound of my own.
The beasts that roam over the plain
 My form with indifference see;
They are so unacquainted with man,
 Their tameness is shocking to me.

Society, Friendship, and Love,
 Divinely bestow'd upon man,
Oh, had I the wings of a dove,
 How soon would I taste you again!
My sorrows I then might assuage
 In the ways of religion and truth,
Might learn from the wisdom of age,
 And be cheer'd by the sallies of youth.

Ye winds that have made me your sport,
 Convey to this desolate shore
Some cordial endearing report
 Of a land I shall visit no more!

My friends—do they now and then send
  A wish or a thought after me?
Oh, tell me I yet have a friend,
  Though a friend I am never to see.

How fleet is a glance of the mind!
  Compared with the speed of its flight,
The tempest itself lags behind,
  And the swift-wingèd arrows of light.
When I think of my own native land,
  In a moment I seem to be there;
But alas! recollection at hand
  Soon hurries me back to despair.

But the seafowl is gone to her nest,
  The beast is laid down in his lair,
Even here is a season of rest,
  And I to my cabin repair.
There's mercy in every place,
  And mercy, encouraging thought!
Gives even affliction a grace,
  And reconciles man to his lot.

WILLIAM COWPER.

The Homes of England.

I wonder if the English people appreciate "The Homes of England."
It is a stately poem worthy of a Goethe or a Shakespeare.   England
is distinctively a country of homes, pretty, little, humble homes as
well as stately palaces and castles, homes well made of stone or brick
for the most part, and clad with ivy and roses.   Who would not be
proud to have had such a home as Ann Hathaway's humble cottage
or one of the little huts in the Lake District?   The homes of America
are often more palatial, especially in small cities, but the use of wood
in America makes them less substantial than the slate-and-brick houses
of England.   (1749-1835.)

THE stately homes of England!
  How beautiful they stand,
Amidst their tall ancestral trees,
  O'er all the pleasant land!
The deer across their greensward bound
  Through shade and sunny gleam,
And the swan glides past them with the sound
  Of some rejoicing stream.

The merry homes of England!
  Around their hearths by night
What gladsome looks of household love
  Meet in the ruddy light!
There woman's voice flows forth in song,
  Or childish tale is told,
Or lips move tunefully along
  Some glorious page of old.

The blessèd homes of England!
  How softly on their bowers
Is laid the holy quietness
  That breathes from Sabbath hours!
Solemn, yet sweet, the church-bell's chime
  Floats through their woods at morn;

All other sounds, in that still time,
    Of breeze and leaf are born.

The cottage homes of England!
    By thousands on her plains,
They are smiling o'er the silvery brooks,
    And round the hamlets' fanes.
Through glowing orchards forth they peep,
    Each from its nook of leaves;
And fearless there the lowly sleep,
    As the bird beneath their eaves.

The free, fair homes of England!
    Long, long, in hut and hall
May hearts of native proof be reared
    To guard each hallowed wall!
And green forever be the groves,
    And bright the flowery sod,
Where first the child's glad spirit loves
    Its country and its God!

                        FELICIA HEMANS.

Horatius at the Bridge.

"Horatius at the Bridge" is too long a poem for children to memorise. But I never saw a boy who did not want some stanzas of it. "Hold the bridge with me!" Boys like that motto instinctively. T. B. Macaulay (1800-59).

LARS PORSENA of Clusium,
    By the Nine Gods he swore
That the great house of Tarquin
    Should suffer wrong no more.
By the Nine Gods he swore it,
    And named a trysting-day,

And bade his messengers ride forth,
East and west and south and north,
  To summon his array.

East and west and south and north
  The messengers ride fast,
And tower and town and cottage
  Have heard the trumpet's blast.
Shame on the false Etruscan
  Who lingers in his home
When Porsena of Clusium
  Is on the march for Rome!

The horsemen and the footmen
  Are pouring in amain,
From many a stately market-place,
  From many a fruitful plain;
From many a lonely hamlet,
  Which, hid by beech and pine,
Like an eagle's nest, hangs on the crest
  Of purple Apennine.

The harvests of Arretium,
  This year, old men shall reap;
This year, young boys in Umbro
  Shall plunge the struggling sheep;
And in the vats of Luna,
  This year, the must shall foam
Round the white feet of laughing girls
  Whose sires have marched to Rome.

There be thirty chosen prophets,
  The wisest of the land,

Who alway by Lars Porsena
  Both morn and evening stand:
Evening and morn the Thirty
  Have turned the verses o'er,
Traced from the right on linen white
  By mighty seers of yore.

And with one voice the Thirty
  Have their glad answer given:
"Go forth, go forth, Lars Porsena;
  Go forth, beloved of Heaven;
Go, and return in glory
  To Clusium's royal dome;
And hang round Nurscia's altars
  The golden shields of Rome."

And now hath every city
  Sent up her tale of men;
The foot are fourscore thousand,
  The horse are thousands ten.
Before the gates of Sutrium
  Is met the great array.
A proud man was Lars Porsena
  Upon the trysting-day.

For all the Etruscan armies
  Were ranged beneath his eye,
And many a banished Roman,
  And many a stout ally;
And with a mighty following
  To join the muster came
The Tusculan Mamilius,
  Prince of the Latian name.

But by the yellow Tiber
  Was tumult and affright:
From all the spacious champaign
  To Rome men took their flight.
A mile around the city,
  The throng stopped up the ways;
A fearful sight it was to see
  Through two long nights and days.

Now, from the rock Tarpeian,
  Could the wan burghers spy
The line of blazing villages
  Red in the midnight sky.
The Fathers of the City,
  They sat all night and day,
For every hour some horseman came
  With tidings of dismay.

To eastward and to westward
  Have spread the Tuscan bands;
Nor house, nor fence, nor dovecot,
  In Crustumerium stands.
Verbenna down to Ostia
  Hath wasted all the plain;
Astur hath stormed Janiculum,
  And the stout guards are slain.

I wis, in all the Senate,
  There was no heart so bold,
But sore it ached, and fast it beat,
  When that ill news was told.
Forthwith up rose the Consul,
  Up rose the Fathers all;

In haste they girded up their gowns,
    And hied them to the wall.

They held a council standing
    Before the River Gate;
Short time was there, ye well may guess,
    For musing or debate.
Out spoke the Consul roundly:
    "The bridge must straight go down;
For, since Janiculum is lost,
    Naught else can save the town."

Just then a scout came flying,
    All wild with haste and fear:
"To arms! to arms! Sir Consul;
    Lars Porsena is here."
On the low hills to westward
    The Consul fixed his eye,
And saw the swarthy storm of dust
    Rise fast along the sky.

And nearer, fast, and nearer
    Doth the red whirlwind come;
And louder still, and still more loud,
From underneath that rolling cloud,
Is heard the trumpet's war-note proud,
    The trampling and the hum.
And plainly and more plainly
    Now through the gloom appears,
Far to left and far to right,
In broken gleams of dark-blue light,
The long array of helmets bright,
    The long array of spears.

And plainly and more plainly,
    Above the glimmering line,
Now might ye see the banners
    Of twelve fair cities shine;
But the banner of proud Clusium
    Was the highest of them all,
The terror of the Umbrian,
    The terror of the Gaul.

Fast by the royal standard,
    O'erlooking all the war,
Lars Porsena of Clusium
    Sat in his ivory car.
By the right wheel rode Mamilius,
    Prince of the Latian name,
And by the left false Sextus,
    That wrought the deed of shame.

But when the face of Sextus
    Was seen among the foes,
A yell that rent the firmament
    From all the town arose.
On the house-tops was no woman
    But spat toward him and hissed,
No child but screamed out curses,
    And shook its little fist.

But the Consul's brow was sad,
    And the Consul's speech was low,
And darkly looked he at the wall,
    And darkly at the foe.
"Their van will be upon us
    Before the bridge goes down;

And if they once may win the bridge,
    What hope to save the town?"

Then out spake brave Horatius,
    The Captain of the Gate:
"To every man upon this earth
    Death cometh soon or late;
And how can man die better
    Than facing fearful odds,
For the ashes of his fathers,
    And the temples of his gods,

"And for the tender mother
    Who dandled him to rest,
And for the wife who nurses
    His baby at her breast,
And for the holy maidens
    Who feed the eternal flame,
To save them from false Sextus
    That wrought the deed of shame?

"Hew down the bridge, Sir Consul,
    With all the speed ye may;
I, with two more to help me,
    Will hold the foe in play.
In yon straight path a thousand
    May well be stopped by three.
Now who will stand on either hand,
    And keep the bridge with me?"

Then out spake Spurius Lartius—
    A Ramnian proud was he—
"Lo, I will stand at thy right hand,
    And keep the bridge with thee.`

And out spake strong Herminius—
  Of Titian blood was he—
"I will abide on thy left side,
  And keep the bridge with thee."

"Horatius," quoth the Consul,
  "As thou say'st, so let it be."
And straight against that great array
  Forth went the dauntless Three.
For Romans in Rome's quarrel
  Spared neither land nor gold,
Nor son nor wife, nor limb nor life,
  In the brave days of old.

Now while the Three were tightening
  Their harness on their backs,
The Consul was the foremost man
  To take in hand an ax;
And Fathers mixed with Commons
  Seized hatchet, bar, and crow,
And smote upon the planks above,
  And loosed the props below.
Meanwhile the Tuscan army,
  Right glorious to behold,
Came flashing back the noonday light,
Rank behind rank, like surges bright
  Of a broad sea of gold.

Four hundred trumpets sounded
  A peal of warlike glee,
As that great host, with measured tread,
And spears advanced, and ensigns spread,
Rolled slowly toward the bridge's head,
  Where stood the dauntless Three.

The Three stood calm and silent,
　And looked upon the foes,
And a great shout of laughter
　From all the vanguard rose:
And forth three chiefs came spurring
　Before that deep array;
To earth they sprang, their swords they
　　drew,
And lifted high their shields, and flew
　To win the narrow way;

Aunus from green Tifernum,
　Lord of the Hill of Vines;
And Seius, whose eight hundred slaves
　Sicken in Ilva's mines;
And Picus, long to Clusium
　Vassal in peace and war,
Who led to fight his Umbrian powers
From that gray crag where, girt with towers,
The fortress of Nequinum lowers
　O'er the pale waves of Nar.

Stout Lartius hurled down Aunus
　Into the stream beneath;
Herminius struck at Seius,
　And clove him to the teeth;
At Picus brave Horatius
　Darted one fiery thrust;
And the proud Umbrian's gilded arms
　Clashed in the bloody dust.

Then Ocnus of Falerii
　Rushed on the Roman Three;

And Lausulus of Urgo,
   The rover of the sea;
And Aruns of Volsinium,
   Who slew the great wild boar,
The great wild boar that had his den
Amid the reeds of Cosa's fen,
And wasted fields and slaughtered men
   Along Albinia's shore.

Herminius smote down Aruns;
   Lartius laid Ocnus low;
Right to the heart of Lausulus
   Horatius sent a blow.
"Lie there," he cried, "fell pirate!
   No more, aghast and pale,
From Ostia's walls the crowd shall mark
The track of thy destroying bark.
No more Campania's hinds shall fly
To woods and caverns when they spy
   Thy thrice accursèd sail."

But now no sound of laughter
   Was heard among the foes.
A wild and wrathful clamour
   From all the vanguard rose.
Six spears' length from the entrance
   Halted that deep array,
And for a space no man came forth
   To win the narrow way.

But hark! the cry is Astur:
   And lo! the ranks divide;
And the great Lord of Luna
   Comes with his stately stride.

Upon his ample shoulders
  Clangs loud the fourfold shield,
And in his hand he shakes the brand
  Which none but he can wield.

He smiled on those bold Romans,
  A smile serene and high;
He eyed the flinching Tuscans,
  And scorn was in his eye.
Quoth he: "The she-wolf's litter
  Stand savagely at bay;
But will ye dare to follow,
  If Astur clears the way?"

Then, whirling up his broadsword
  With both hands to the height,
He rushed against Horatius,
  And smote with all his might.
With shield and blade Horatius
  Right deftly turned the blow.
The blow, though turned, came yet too nigh;
It missed his helm, but gashed his thigh:
The Tuscans raised a joyful cry
  To see the red blood flow.

He reeled, and on Herminius
  He leaned one breathing space;
Then, like a wildcat mad with wounds,
  Sprang right at Astur's face.
Through teeth, and skull, and helmet,
  So fierce a thrust he sped,
The good sword stood a handbreadth out
  Behind the Tuscan's head.

And the great Lord of Luna
　　Fell at the deadly stroke,
As falls on Mount Alvernus
　　A thunder-smitten oak.
Far o'er the crashing forest
　　The giant arms lie spread;
And the pale augurs, muttering low,
　　Gaze on the blasted head.

On Astur's throat Horatius
　　Right firmly pressed his heel,
And thrice and four times tugged amain
　　Ere he wrenched out the steel.
"And see," he cried, "the welcome,
　　Fair guests, that waits you here!
What noble Lucumo comes next
　　To taste our Roman cheer?"

But at his haughty challenge
　　A sullen murmur ran,
Mingled of wrath, and shame, and dread,
　　Along that glittering van.
There lacked not men of prowess,
　　Nor men of lordly race;
For all Etruria's noblest
　　Were round the fatal place.

But all Etruria's noblest
　　Felt their hearts sink t see
On the earth the bloody corpses,
　　In the path the dauntless Three:
And, from the ghastly entrance
　　Where those bold Romans stood,

All shrank, like boys who unaware,
Ranging the woods to start a hare,
Come to the mouth of the dark lair
Where, growling low, a fierce old bear
    Lies amid bones and blood.

Was none who would be foremost
    To lead such dire attack?
But those behind cried "Forward!"
    And those before cried "Back!"
And backward now and forward
    Wavers the deep array;
And on the tossing sea of steel
To and fro the standards reel;
And the victorious trumpet peal
    Dies fitfully away.

Yet one man for one moment
    Strode out before the crowd;
Well known was he to all the Three,
' And they gave him greeting loud:
"Now welcome, welcome, Sextus!
    Now welcome to thy home!
Why dost thou stay, and turn away?
    Here lies the road to Rome."

Thrice looked he at the city;
    Thrice looked he at the dead;
And thrice came on in fury,
    And thrice turned back in dread:
And, white with fear and hatred,
    Scowled at the narrow way
Where, wallowing in a pool of blood,
    The bravest Tuscans lay.

But meanwhile ax and lever
   Have manfully been plied,
And now the bridge hangs tottering
   Above the boiling tide.
"Come back, come back, Horatius!"
   Loud cried the Fathers all.
"Back, Lartius! Back, Herminius!
   Back, ere the ruin fall!"

Back darted Spurius Lartius;
   Herminius darted back:
And, as they passed, beneath their feet
   They felt the timbers crack.
But when they turned their faces,
   And on the farther shore
Saw brave Horatius stand alone,
   They would have crossed once more.

But with a crash like thunder
   Fell every loosened beam,
And, like a dam, the mighty wreck
   Lay right athwart the stream;
And a long shout of triumph
   Rose from the walls of Rome,
As to the highest turret tops
   Was splashed the yellow foam.

And, like a horse unbroken
   When first he feels the rein,
The furious river struggled hard,
   And tossed his tawny mane;
And burst the curb, and bounded,
   Rejoicing to be free,

And whirling down, in fierce career,
Battlement, and plank, and pier,
  Rushed headlong to the sea.

Alone stood brave Horatius,
  But constant still in mind;
Thrice thirty thousand foes before,
  And the broad flood behind.
"Down with him!" cried false Sextus,
  With a smile on his pale face.
"Now yield thee," cried Lars Porsena,
  "Now yield thee to our grace."

Round turned he, as not deigning
  Those craven ranks to see;
Naught spake he to Lars Porsena,
  To Sextus naught spake he;
But he saw on Palatinus
  The white porch of his home;
And he spake to the noble river
  That rolls by the towers of Rome:

"O Tiber! Father Tiber!
  To whom the Romans pray,
A Roman's life, a Roman's arms,
  Take thou in charge this day!"
So he spake, and speaking sheathed
  The good sword by his side,
And, with his harness on his back,
  Plunged headlong in the tide.

No sound of joy or sorrow
  Was heard from either bank;

But friends and foes in dumb surprise,
With parted lips and straining eyes,
  Stood gazing where he sank;
And when above the surges
  They saw his crest appear,
All Rome sent forth a rapturous cry,
And even the ranks of Tuscany
  Could scarce forbear to cheer.

And fiercely ran the current,
  Swollen high by months of rain;
And fast his blood was flowing,
  And he was sore in pain,
And heavy with his armour,
  And spent with changing blows:
And oft they thought him sinking,
  But still again he rose.

Never, I ween, did swimmer,
  In such an evil case,
Struggle through such a raging flood
  Safe to the landing place;
But his limbs were borne up bravely
  By the brave heart within,
And our good Father Tiber
  Bore bravely up his chin.

"Curse on him!" quoth false Sextus;
  "Will not the villain drown?
But for this stay, ere close of day
  We should have sacked the town!"
"Heaven help him!" quoth Lars Porsena,
  "And bring him safe to shore;

For such a gallant feat of arms
   Was never seen before."

And now he feels the bottom;
   Now on dry earth he stands;
Now round him throng the Fathers
   To press his gory hands;
And now with shouts and clapping,
   And noise of weeping loud,
He enters through the River Gate,
   Borne by the joyous crowd.

They gave him of the corn land,
   That was of public right,
As much as two strong oxen
   Could plow from morn till night:
And they made a molten image,
   And set it up on high,
And there it stands unto this day
   To witness if I lie.

It stands in the Comitium,
   Plain for all folk to see,—
Horatius in his harness,
   Halting upon one knee:
And underneath is written,
   In letters all of gold,
How valiantly he kept the bridge
   In the brave days of old.

And still his name sounds stirring
   Unto the men of Rome,
As the trumpet blast that cries to them
   To charge the Volscian home;

And wives still pray to Juno
  For boys with hearts as bold
As his who kept the bridge so well
  In the brave days of old.

And in the nights of winter,
  When the cold north winds blow,
And the long howling of the wolves
  Is heard amid the snow;
When round the lonely cottage
  Roars loud the tempest's din,
And the good logs of Algidus
  Roar louder yet within;

When the oldest cask is opened,
  And the largest lamp is lit;
When the chestnuts glow in the embers,
  And the kid turns on the spit;
When young and old in circle
  Around the firebrands close;
When the girls are weaving baskets,
  And the lads are shaping bows;

When the goodman mends his armour,
  And trims his helmet's plume;
When the goodwife's shuttle merrily
  Goes flashing through the loom,—
With weeping and with laughter
  Still is the story told,
How well Horatius kept the bridge
  In the brave days of old.

THOMAS B. MACAULAY.

The Planting of the Apple-Tree.

"The Planting of the Apple-Tree" has become a favourite for "Arbour Day" exercises. The planting of trees as against their destruction is a vital point in our political and national welfare. William Cullen Bryant (1794–1878).

COME, let us plant the apple-tree.
Cleave the tough greensward with the spade;
Wide let its hollow bed be made;
There gently lay the roots, and there
Sift the dark mould with kindly care,
 And press it o'er them tenderly,
As round the sleeping infant's feet
We softly fold the cradle sheet;
 So plant we the apple-tree.

What plant we in this apple-tree?
Buds, which the breath of summer days
Shall lengthen into leafy sprays;
Boughs where the thrush, with crimson breast,
Shall haunt, and sing, and hide her nest;
 We plant, upon the sunny lea,
A shadow for the noontide hour,
A shelter from the summer shower,
 When we plant the apple-tree.

What plant we in this apple-tree?
Sweets for a hundred flowery springs,
To load the May wind's restless wings,
When, from the orchard row, he pours
Its fragrance through our open doors;
 A world of blossoms for the bee,
Flowers for the sick girl's silent room,
For the glad infant sprigs of bloom,
 We plant with the apple-tree.

What plant we in this apple-tree?
Fruits that shall swell in sunny June,
And redden in the August noon,
And drop, when gentle airs come by,
That fan the blue September sky,
   While children come, with cries of glee,
And seek them where the fragrant grass
Betrays their bed to those who pass,
   At the foot of the apple-tree.

And when, above this apple-tree,
The winter stars are quivering bright,
The winds go howling through the night,
Girls, whose eyes o'erflow with mirth,
Shall peel its fruit by cottage hearth,
   And guests in prouder homes shall see,
Heaped with the grape of Cintra's vine,
And golden orange of the line,
   The fruit of the apple-tree.

The fruitage of this apple-tree,
Winds and our flag of stripe and star
Shall bear to coasts that lie afar,
Where men shall wonder at the view,
And ask in what fair groves they grew;
   And sojourners beyond the sea
Shall think of childhood's careless day,
And long, long hours of summer play,
   In the shade of the apple-tree.

Each year shall give this apple-tree
A broader flush of roseate bloom,
A deeper maze of verdurous gloom,

And loosen, when the frost-clouds lower,
The crisp brown leaves in thicker shower.
   The years shall come and pass, but we
Shall hear no longer, where we lie,
The summer's songs, the autumn's sigh,
   In the boughs of the apple-tree.

And time shall waste this apple-tree.
Oh, when its aged branches throw
Thin shadows on the ground below,
Shall fraud and force and iron will
Oppress the weak and helpless still?
   What shall the tasks of mercy be,
Amid the toils, the strifes, the tears
Of those who live when length of years
   Is wasting this apple-tree?

"Who planted this old apple-tree?"
The children of that distant day
Thus to some aged man shall say;
And, gazing on its mossy stem,
The gray-haired man shall answer them:
   "A poet of the land was he,
Born in the rude but good old times;
'Tis said he made some quaint old rhymes
   On planting the apple-tree."
                    WILLIAM CULLEN BRYANT.

PART V.

On and On

PART V

June.

"June" (by James Russell Lowell, 1819-91) is a fragment from "The Vision of Sir Launfal." It finds a place in this volume because it is the most perfect description of a charming day ever written.

WHAT is so rare as a day in June?
Then, if ever, come perfect days;
Then Heaven tries the earth if it be in tune,
    And over it softly her warm ear lays:
Whether we look, or whether we listen,
We hear life murmur, or see it glisten;
Every clod feels a stir of might,
    An instinct within it that reaches and towers,
And, groping blindly above it for light,
    Climbs to a soul in grass and flowers;
The flush of life may well be seen
    Thrilling back over hills and valleys;
The cowslip startles in meadows green,
    The buttercup catches the sun in its chalice,
And there's never a leaf nor a blade too mean
    To be some happy creature's palace;
The little bird sits at his door in the sun,
    Atilt like a blossom among the leaves,
And lets his illumined being o'errun
    With the deluge of summer it receives;
His mate feels the eggs beneath her wings,
And the heart in her dumb breast flutters and sings;
He sings to the wide world, and she to her nest,—
In the nice ear of Nature which song is the best?
                JAMES RUSSELL LOWELL.

A Psalm of Life.

WHAT THE HEART OF THE YOUNG MAN SAID TO THE PSALMIST.

"A Psalm of Life," by Henry W. Longfellow (1807–82), is like a treasure laid up in heaven. It should be learned for its future value to the child, not necessarily because the child likes it. Its value will dawn on him.

TELL me not, in mournful numbers,
    Life is but an empty dream!—
For the soul is dead that slumbers,
    And things are not what they seem.

Life is real! Life is earnest!
    And the grave is not its goal;
Dust thou art, to dust returnest,
    Was not spoken of the soul.

Not enjoyment, and not sorrow,
    Is our destined end or way;
But to act, that each to-morrow
    Find us farther than to-day.

Art is long, and Time is fleeting,
    And our hearts, though stout and brave,
Still, like muffled drums, are beating
    Funeral marches to the grave.

In the world's broad field of battle,
    In the bivouac of Life,
Be not like dumb, driven cattle!
    Be a hero in the strife!

Trust no Future, howe'er pleasant!
　　Let the dead Past bury its dead!
Act,—act in the living Present!
　　· Heart within, and God o'erhead!

Lives of great men all remind us
　　We can make our lives sublime,
And, departing, leave behind us
　　Footprints on the sands of time;

Footprints, that perhaps another,
　　Sailing o'er life's solemn main,
A forlorn and shipwrecked brother,
　　Seeing, shall take heart again.

Let us, then, be up and doing,
　　With a heart for any fate;
Still achieving, still pursuing,
　　Learn to labour and to wait.

HENRY W. LONGFELLOW.

Barnacles.

"Barnacles" (by Sidney Lanier, 1842–81) is a poem that I teach in connection with my lessons on natural history. We have a good specimen of a barnacle, and the children see them on the shells on the coast. The ethical point is invaluable.

My soul is sailing through the sea,
But the Past is heavy and hindereth me.
The Past hath crusted cumbrous shells
That hold the flesh of cold sea-mells
　　About my soul.
The huge waves wash, the high waves roll,
Each barnacle clingeth and worketh dole
　　And hindereth me from sailing!

Old Past, let go, and drop i' the sea
Till fathomless waters cover thee!
For I am living, but thou art dead;
Thou drawest back, I strive ahead
      The Day to find.
Thy shells unbind!   Night comes behind;
I needs must hurry with the wind
      And trim me best for sailing.
              SIDNEY LANIER.

A Happy Life.

How happy is he born and taught
   That serveth not another's will;
Whose armour is his honest thought,
   And simple truth his utmost skill!

Whose passions not his master's are,
   Whose soul is still prepared for death,
Not tied unto the world with care
   Of public fame, or private breath.
             SIR HENRY WOTTON.

Home, Sweet Home!

"Home, Sweet Home" (John Howard Payne, 1791–1852) is a poem
that reaches into the heart. What is home? A place where we ex-
perience independence, safety, privacy, and where we can dispense
hospitality. "The family is the true unit."

'MID pleasures and palaces though we may roam,
Be it ever so humble, there's no place like
   home;

A charm from the sky seems to hallow us there,
Which, seek through the world, is ne'er met with
    elsewhere.
        Home! Home! sweet, sweet Home!
There's no place like Home! there's no place like
    Home!

An exile from Home, splendour dazzles in vain;
O, give me my lowly thatched cottage again!
The birds singing gaily, that came at my call,—
Give me them,—and the peace of mind, dearer
    than all!
        Home! Home! sweet, sweet Home!
There's no place like Home! there's no place like
    Home!

How sweet 'tis to sit 'neath a fond father's smile,
And the cares of a mother to soothe and beguile!
Let others delight 'mid new pleasures to roam,
But give me, oh, give me, the pleasures of Home!
        Home! Home! sweet, sweet Home!
There's no place like Home! there's no place like
    Home!

To thee I'll return, overburdened with care;
The heart's dearest solace will smile on me there;
No more from that cottage again will I roam;
Be it ever so humble, there's no place like Home.
        Home! Home! sweet, sweet Home!
There's no place like Home! there's no place like
    Home!

                JOHN HOWARD PAYNE.

From Casa Guidi Windows.

JULIET OF NATIONS.

I HEARD last night a little child go singing
　'Neath Casa Guidi windows, by the church,
O bella libertà, O bella !—stringing
　The same words still on notes he went in search
So high for, you concluded the upspringing
　Of such a nimble bird to sky from perch
Must leave the whole bush in a tremble green,
　And that the heart of Italy must beat,
While such a voice had leave to rise serene
　'Twixt church and palace of a Florence street:
A little child, too, who not long had been
　By mother's finger steadied on his feet,
And still *O bella libertà* he sang.

ELIZABETH BARRETT BROWNING.

Woodman, Spare That Tree !

"Woodman, Spare That Tree" (by George Pope Morris, 1802-64) is included in this collection because I have loved it all my life, and I never knew any one who could or would offer a criticism upon it. Its value lies in its recognition of childhood's pleasures.

WOODMAN, spare that tree !
　Touch not a single bough !
In youth it sheltered me,
　And I'll protect it now.
'Twas my forefather's hand
　That placed it near his cot;
There, woodman, let it stand,
　Thy ax shall harm it not.

That old familiar tree,
  Whose glory and renown
Are spread o'er land and sea—
  And wouldst thou hew it down?
Woodman, forbear thy stroke!
  Cut not its earth-bound ties;
Oh, spare that agèd oak
  Now towering to the skies!

When but an idle boy,
  I sought its grateful shade;
In all their gushing joy
  Here, too, my sisters played.
My mother kissed me here;
  My father pressed my hand—
Forgive this foolish tear,
  But let that old oak stand.

My heart-strings round thee cling,
  Close as thy bark, old friend!
Here shall the wild-bird sing,
  And still thy branches bend.
Old tree! the storm still brave!
  And, woodman, leave the spot;
While I've a hand to save,
  Thy ax shall harm it not.
                    GEORGE POPE MORRIS.

Abide With Me.

"Abide With Me" (Henry Francis Lyte, 1793-1847) appeals to
our natural longing for the unchanging and to our love of security.

ABIDE with me! fast falls the eventide;
The darkness deepens; Lord, with me abide!

When other helpers fail, and comforts flee,
Help of the helpless, O abide with me.

Swift to its close ebbs out life's little day;
Earth's joys grow dim, its glories pass away;
Change and decay in all around I see:
O Thou who changest not, abide with me!

HENRY FRANCIS LYTE.

Lead, Kindly Light.

"Lead, Kindly Light," by John Henry Newman (1801-90), was written when Cardinal Newman was in the stress and strain of perplexity and mental distress and bodily pain. The poem has been a star in the darkness to thousands. It was the favourite poem of President McKinley.

LEAD, kindly Light, amid th' encircling gloom,
       Lead Thou me on;
The night is dark, and I am far from home,
       Lead Thou me on.
Keep Thou my feet; I do not ask to see
The distant scene; one step enough for me.

I was not ever thus, nor prayed that Thou
       Shouldst lead me on;
I loved to choose and see my path; but now
       Lead Thou me on.
I loved the garish day; and, spite of fears,
Pride ruled my will: remember not past years.

So long Thy power hath blest me, sure it still
       Will lead me on
O'er moor and fen, o'er crag and torrent, till
       The night is gone,

And with the morn those angel faces smile,
Which I have loved long since, and lost a while.
JOHN HENRY NEWMAN.

The Last Rose of Summer.

'Tis the last rose of summer
    Left blooming alone;
All her lovely companions
    Are faded and gone;
No flower of her kindred,
    No rose-bud is nigh,
To reflect back her blushes,
    Or give sigh for sigh.

I'll not leave thee, thou lone one!
    To pine on the stem;
Since the lovely are sleeping,
    Go, sleep thou with them.
Thus kindly I scatter
    Thy leaves o'er the bed
Where thy mates of the garden
    Lie scentless and dead.

So soon may I follow,
    When friendships decay,
And from Love's shining circle
    The gems drop away.
When true hearts lie withered,
    And fond ones are flown,
O! who would inhabit
    This bleak world alone?
THOMAS MOORE.

Annie Laurie.

"Annie Laurie" finds a place in this collection because it is the most popular song on earth.   Written by William Douglas (————).

MAXWELTON braes are bonnie
Where early fa's the dew,
And it's there that Annie Laurie
Gie'd me her promise true—
Gie'd me her promise true,
Which ne'er forgot will be;
And for bonnie Annie Laurie
I'd lay me doune and dee.

Her brow is like the snawdrift,
Her throat is like the swan,
Her face it is the fairest
That e'er the sun shone on—
That e'er the sun shone on;
And dark blue is her e'e;
And for bonnie Annie Laurie
I'd lay me doune and dee.

Like dew on the gowan lying
Is the fa' o' her fairy feet;
Like the winds in summer sighing,
Her voice is low and sweet—
Her voice is low and sweet;
And she's a' the world to me;
And for bonnie Annie Laurie
I'd lay me doune and dee.

WILLIAM DOUGLAS.

The Ship of State.

A president of a well-known college writes me that "The Ship of State" was his favourite poem when he was a boy, and did more than any other to shape his course in life.   Longfellow (1807–82).

SAIL on, sail on, O Ship of State!
Sail on, O Union, strong and great!
Humanity, with all its fears,
With all the hopes of future years,
Is hanging breathless on thy fate!
We know what Master laid thy keel,
What Workmen wrought thy ribs of steel,
Who made each mast, and sail, and rope;
What anvils rang, what hammers beat,
In what a forge and what a heat
Were forged the anchors of thy hope!
Fear not each sudden sound and shock—
'Tis of the wave, and not the rock;
'Tis but the flapping of the sail,
And not a rent made by the gale!
In spite of rock, and tempest roar,
In spite of false lights on the shore,
Sail on, nor fear to breast the sea!
Our hearts, our hopes, are all with thee.
Our hearts, our hopes, our prayers, our tears,
Our faith, triumphant o'er our fears,
Are all with thee, are all with thee!

HENRY W. LONGFELLOW.

The Constitution and Laws are here personified, and addressed as "The Ship of State."

America.

"America" (Samuel Francis Smith, 1808–95) is a good poem to learn as a poem, regardless of the fact that every American who can sing it ought to know it, that he may join in the chorus when patriotic celebrations call for it. My boys love to repeat the entire poem, but I often find masses of people trying to sing it, knowing only one stanza. It is our national anthem, and a part of our education to know every word of it.

My country, 'tis of thee,
Sweet land of liberty,
   Of thee I sing;
Land where my fathers died,
Land of the Pilgrims' pride;
From every mountain side,
   Let freedom ring.

My native country, thee—
Land of the noble free—
   Thy name I love;
I love thy rocks and rills,
Thy woods and templed hills;
My heart with rapture thrills,
   Like that above.

Let music swell the breeze,
And ring from all the trees
   Sweet freedom's song;
Let mortal tongues awake;
Let all that breathe partake;
Let rocks their silence break—
   The sound prolong.

Our fathers' God, to Thee,
Author of liberty,
   To Thee we sing;

Long may our land be bright
With freedom's holy light:
Protect us by Thy might,
  Great God, our King.

                              S. F. SMITH.

The Landing of the Pilgrims.

"The Landing of the Pilgrims," by Felicia Hemans (1749–1835), is a poem that children want when they study the early history of America.

THE breaking waves dashed high
  On a stern and rock-bound coast,
And the woods against a stormy sky
  Their giant branches tossed.

And the heavy night hung dark
  The hills and waters o'er,
When a band of exiles moored their bark
  On the wild New England shore.

Not as the conqueror comes,
  They, the true-hearted, came;
Not with the roll of the stirring drums,
  And the trumpet that sings of fame.

Not as the flying come,
  In silence and in fear;
They shook the depths of the desert gloom
  With their hymns of lofty cheer.

Amid the storm they sang,
  And the stars heard, and the sea:
And the sounding aisles of the dim woods rang
  To the anthem of the free !

The ocean eagle soared
  From his nest by the white wave's foam:
And the rocking pines of the forest roared,—
  This was their welcome home!

There were men with hoary hair,
  Amid that pilgrim band;
Why had *they* come to wither there,
  Away from their childhood's land?

There was woman's fearless eye,
  Lit by her deep love's truth;
There was manhood's brow serenely high,
  And the fiery heart of youth.

What sought they thus afar?
  Bright jewels of the mine?
The wealth of seas, the spoils of war?—
  They sought a faith's pure shrine!

Ay! call it holy ground,
  The soil where first they trod:
They have left unstained what there they
    found,
  Freedom to worship God.

FELICIA HEMANS.

The Lotos-Eaters.

The main idea in "The Lotus-Eaters" is, are we justified in running away from unpleasant duties? Or, is insensibility justifiable?

Laddie, do you recollect learning this poem after we had read the story of "Odysseus"? "The struggle of the soul urged to action, but held back by the spirit of self-indulgence." These were the points we discussed. Alfred Tennyson (1809–92).

"Courage!" he said, and pointed toward the land,
"This mounting wave will roll us shoreward
    soon."
In the afternoon they came unto a land
In which it seemèd always afternoon.
All round the coast the languid air did swoon,
Breathing like one that hath a weary dream.
Full-faced above the valley stood the moon;
And like a downward smoke, the slender stream
Along the cliff to fall and pause and fall did seem.

A land of streams! some, like a downward smoke,
Slow-dropping veils of thinnest lawn, did go;
And some thro' wavering lights and shadows broke,
Rolling a slumbrous sheet of foam below.
They saw the gleaming river seaward flow
From the inner land: far off, three mountain-
    tops,
Three silent pinnacles of agèd snow,
Stood sunset-flush'd: and, dew'd with showery
    drops,
Up-clomb the shadowy pine above the woven
    copse.

The charmèd sunset linger'd low adown
In the red West: thro' mountain clefts the dale

Was seen far inland, and the yellow down
Border'd with palm, and many a winding vale
And meadow, set with slender galingale;
A land where all things always seem'd the same!
And round about the keel with faces pale,
Dark faces pale against that rosy flame,
The mild-eyed melancholy Lotos-eaters came.

Branches they bore of that enchanted stem,
Laden with flower and fruit, whereof they gave
To each, but whoso did receive of them,
And taste, to him the gushing of the wave
Far, far away did seem to mourn and rave
On alien shores; and if his fellow spake,
His voice was thin, as voices from the grave;
And deep-asleep he seem'd, yet all awake,
And music in his ears his beating heart did make.

They sat them down upon the yellow sand,
Between the sun and moon upon the shore;
And sweet it was to dream of Fatherland,
Of child, and wife, and slave; but evermore
Most weary seem'd the sea, weary the oar,
Weary the wandering fields of barren foam.
Then some one said, "We will return no more;"
And all at once they sang, "Our island home
Is far beyond the wave; we will no longer roam."

ALFRED TENNYSON.

Moly.

"Moly" (mo'ly), by Edith M. Thomas (1850-), is the best pos-
sible presentation of the value of integrity. This poem ranks with
"Sir Galahad," if not above it. It is a stroke of genius, and every
American ought to be proud of it. Every time my boys read "Odysseus"
or the story of Ulysses with me we read or learn "Moly." The plant
moly grows in the United States as well as in Europe.

TRAVELLER, pluck a stem of moly,
If thou touch at Circe's isle,—
Hermes' moly, growing solely
To undo enchanter's wile!
When she proffers thee her chalice,—
Wine and spices mixed with malice,—
When she smites thee with her staff
To transform thee, do thou laugh!
Safe thou art if thou but bear
The least leaf of moly rare.
Close it grows beside her portal,
Springing from a stock immortal,
Yes! and often has the Witch
Sought to tear it from its niche;
But to thwart her cruel will
The wise God renews it still.
Though it grows in soil perverse,
Heaven hath been its jealous nurse,
And a flower of snowy mark
Springs from root and sheathing dark;
Kingly safeguard, only herb
That can brutish passion curb!
Some do think its name should be
Shield-Heart, White Integrity.
Traveller, pluck a stem of moly,
If thou touch at Circe's isle,—

Hermes' moly, growing solely
To undo enchanter's wile!

EDITH M. THOMAS.

Cupid Drowned.

"Cupid Drowned" (1784–1859), "Cupid Stung" (1779–1852), and "Cupid and My Campasbe" (1558–1606) are three dainty poems recommended by Mrs. Margaret Mooney, of the Albany Teachers' College, in her "Foundation Studies in Literature." Children are always delighted with them.

T'OTHER day as I was twining
Roses, for a crown to dine in,
What, of all things, 'mid the heap,
Should I light on, fast asleep,
But the little desperate elf,
The tiny traitor, Love, himself!
By the wings I picked him up
Like a bee, and in a cup
Of my wine I plunged and sank him,
Then what d'ye think I did?—I drank him.
Faith, I thought him dead. Not he!
There he lives with tenfold glee;
And now this moment with his wings
I feel him tickling my heart-strings.

LEIGH HUNT.

Cupid Stung.

CUPID once upon a bed
Of roses laid his weary head;
Luckless urchin, not to see
Within the leaves a slumbering bee.
The bee awak'd—with anger wild
The bee awak'd, and stung the child.

Loud and piteous are his cries;
To Venus quick he runs, he flies;
"Oh, Mother! I am wounded through—
I die with pain—in sooth I do!
Stung by some little angry thing,
Some serpent on a tiny wing—
A bee it was—for once, I know,
I heard a rustic call it so."
Thus he spoke, and she the while
Heard him with a soothing smile;
Then said, "My infant, if so much
Thou feel the little wild bee's touch,
How must the heart, ah, Cupid! be,
The hapless heart that's stung by thee!"

THOMAS MOORE.

Cupid and My Campasbe.

CUPID and my Campasbe played
At cards for kisses. Cupid paid.
He stakes his quiver, bow and arrows,
His mother's doves and team of sparrows.
Loses them, too; then down he throws
The coral of his lips, the rose
Growing on his cheek, but none knows how;
With them the crystal of his brow,
And then the dimple of his chin.
All these did my Campasbe win.
At last he set her both his eyes;
She won and Cupid blind did rise.
Oh, Love, hath she done this to thee!
What shall, alas, become of me!

JOHN LYLY.

A Ballad for a Boy.

Violo Roseboro, one of our good authors, brought to me "A Ballad for a Boy," saying: "I believe it is one of the poems that every child ought to know." It is included in this compilation out of respect to her opinion and also because the boys to whom I have read it said it was "great." The lesson in it is certainly fine. Men who are true men want to settle their own disputes by a hand-to-hand fight, but they will always help each other when a third party or the elements interfere. Humanity is greater than human interests.

WHEN George the Third was reigning, a hundred
    years ago,
He ordered Captain Farmer to chase the foreign
    foe.
"You're not afraid of shot," said he, "you're not
    afraid of wreck,
So cruise about the west of France in the frigate
    called *Quebec*.

"Quebec was once a Frenchman's town, but
    twenty years ago
King George the Second sent a man called General
    Wolfe, you know,
To clamber up a precipice and look into Quebec,
As you'd look down a hatchway when standing
    on the deck.

"If Wolfe could beat the Frenchmen then, so
    you can beat them now.
Before he got inside the town he died, I must
    allow.
But since the town was won for us it is a lucky
    name,
And you'll remember Wolfe's good work, and
    you shall do the same."

Then Farmer said, "I'll try, sir," and Farmer
    bowed so low
That George could see his pigtail tied in a velvet bow.
George gave him his commission, and that it
    might be safer,
Signed "King of Britain, King of France," and
    sealed it with a wafer.

Then proud was Captain Farmer in a frigate of
    his own,
And grander on his quarter-deck than George
    upon his throne.
He'd two guns in his cabin, and on the spar-deck ten,
And twenty on the gun-deck, and more than ten-
    score men.

And as a hunstman scours the brakes with sixteen
    brace of dogs,
With two-and-thirty cannon the ship explored the
    fogs.
From Cape la Hogue to Ushant, from Rochefort to
    Belleisle,
She hunted game till reef and mud were rubbing
    on her keel.

The fogs are dried, the frigate's side is bright with
    melting tar,
The lad up in the foretop sees square white sails
    afar;
The east wind drives three square-sailed masts
    from out the Breton bay,
And "Clear for action!" Farmer shouts, and
    reefers yell "Hooray!"

The Frenchmen's captain had a name I wish I
    could pronounce;
A Breton gentleman was he, and wholly free from
    bounce,
One like those famous fellows who died by guil-
    lotine
For honour and the fleur-de-lys, and Antoinette
    the Queen.

The Catholic for Louis, the Protestant for George,
Each captain drew as bright a sword as saintly
    smiths could forge;
And both were simple seamen, but both could
    understand
How each was bound to win or die for flag and
    native land.

The French ship was *La Surveillante*, which means
    the watchful maid;
She folded up her head-dress and began to can-
    nonade.
Her hull was clean, and ours was foul; we had to
    spread more sail.
On canvas, stays, and topsail yards her bullets
    came like hail.

Sore smitten were both captains, and many lads
    beside,
And still to cut our rigging the foreign gunners tried.
A sail-clad spar came flapping down athwart a
    blazing gun;
We could not quench the rushing flames, and so
    the Frenchman won.

Our quarter-deck was crowded, the waist was all
    aglow;
Men hung upon the taffrail half scorched, but
    loth to go;
Our captain sat where once he stood, and would not
    quit his chair.
He bade his comrades leap for life, and leave him
    bleeding there

The guns were hushed on either side, the French-
    men lowered boats,
They flung us planks and hen-coops, and every-
    thing that floats.
They risked their lives, good fellows! to bring
    their rivals aid.
'Twas by the conflagration the peace was strangely
    made.

La Surveillante was like a sieve; the victors had no
    rest;
They had to dodge the east wind to reach the port
    of Brest.
And where the waves leapt lower and the riddled
    ship went slower,
In triumph, yet in funeral guise, came fisher-
    boats to tow her.

They dealt with us as brethren, they mourned for
    Farmer dead;
And as the wounded captives passed each Breton
    bowed the head.

Then spoke the French Lieutenant, "'Twas fire
    that won, not we.
You never struck your flag to us; you'll go to
    England free."

'Twas the sixth day of October, seventeen hundred
    seventy-nine,
A year when nations ventured against us to
    combine,
Quebec was burned and Farmer slain, by us re-
    membered not;
But thanks be to the French book wherein they're
    not forgot.

Now you, if you've to fight the French, my
    youngster, bear in mind
Those seamen of King Louis so chivalrous and kind;
Think of the Breton gentlemen who took our
    lads to Brest,
And treat some rescued Breton as a comrade and
    a guest.

The Skeleton in Armour.

"The Skeleton in Armour" (Longfellow, 1807–82) is a "boys' poem."
It is pure literature and good history.

"SPEAK! speak! thou fearful guest!
    Who, with thy hollow breast
    Still in rude armour drest,
        Comest to daunt me!
    Wrapt not in Eastern balms,
    But with thy fleshless palms
    Stretched, as if asking alms,
        Why dost thou haunt me?"

Then from those cavernous eyes
Pale flashes seemed to rise,
As when the Northern skies
   Gleam in December;
And, like the water's flow
Under December's snow,
Came a dull voice of woe
   From the heart's chamber.

"I was a Viking old!
My deeds, though manifold,
No Skald in song has told,
   No Saga taught thee!
Take heed that in thy verse
Thou dost the tale rehearse,
Else dread a dead man's curse;
   For this I sought thee.

"Far in the Northern Land,
By the wild Baltic's strand,
I, with my childish hand,
   Tamed the gerfalcon;
And, with my skates fast-bound,
Skimmed the half-frozen Sound,
That the poor whimpering hound
   Trembled to walk on.

"Oft to his frozen lair
Tracked I the grizzly bear,
While from my path the hare
   Fled like a shadow;

Oft through the forest dark
Followed the were-wolf's bark,
Until the soaring lark
   Sang from the meadow.

"But when I older grew,
Joining a corsair's crew,
O'er the dark sea I flew
   With the marauders.
Wild was the life we led;
Many the souls that sped,
Many the hearts that bled,
   By our stern orders.

"Many a wassail-bout
Wore the long Winter out;
Often our midnight shout
   Set the cocks crowing,
As we the Berserk's tale
Measured in cups of ale,
Draining the oaken pail
   Filled to o'erflowing.

"Once as I told in glee
Tales of the stormy sea,
Soft eyes did gaze on me,
   Burning yet tender;
And as the white stars shine
On the dark Norway pine,
On that dark heart of mine
   Fell their soft splendour.

"I wooed the blue-eyed maid,
Yielding, yet half afraid,
And in the forest's shade
　Our vows were plighted.
Under its loosened vest
Fluttered her little breast,
Like birds within their nest
　By the hawk frighted.

"Bright in her father's hall
Shields gleamed upon the wall,
Loud sang the minstrels all,
　Chanting his glory;
When of old Hildebrand
I asked his daughter's hand,
Mute did the minstrels stand
　To hear my story.

"While the brown ale he quaffed,
Loud then the champion laughed,
And as the wind-gusts waft
　The sea-foam brightly,
So the loud laugh of scorn,
Out of those lips unshorn,
From the deep drinking-horn
　Blew the foam lightly.

"She was a Prince's child,
I but a Viking wild,
And though she blushed and smiled,
　I was discarded!

Should not the dove so white
Follow the sea-mew's flight?
Why did they leave that night
    Her nest unguarded?

"Scarce had I put to sea,
Bearing the maid with me,—
Fairest of all was she
    Among the Norsemen!—
When on the white sea-strand,
Waving his armèd hand,
Saw we old Hildebrand,
    With twenty horsemen.

"Then launched they to the blast,
Bent like a reed each mast,
Yet we were gaining fast,
    When the wind failed us;
And with a sudden flaw
Came round the gusty Skaw,
So that our foe we saw
    Laugh as he hailed us.

"And as to catch the gale
Round veered the flapping sail,
'Death!' was the helmsman's hail,
    'Death without quarter!'
Midships with iron keel
Struck we her ribs of steel;
Down her black hulk did reel
    Through the black water!

" As with his wings aslant,
Sails the fierce cormorant,
Seeking some rocky haunt,
  With his prey laden,
So toward the open main,
Beating to sea again,
Through the wild hurricane,
  Bore I the maiden.

"Three weeks we westward bore,
And when the storm was o'er,
Cloud-like we saw the shore
  Stretching to leeward;
There for my lady's bower
Built I the lofty tower
Which to this very hour
  Stands looking seaward.

"There lived we many years;
Time dried the maiden's tears;
She had forgot her fears,
  She was a mother;
Death closed her mild blue eyes;
Under that tower she lies;
Ne'er shall the sun arise
  On such another.

"Still grew my bosom then,
Still as a stagnant fen!
Hateful to me were men,
  The sunlight hateful!

In the vast forest here,
Clad in my warlike gear,
Fell I upon my spear,
   Oh, death was grateful!

"Thus, seamed with many scars,
Bursting these prison bars,
Up to its native stars
   My soul ascended!
There from the flowing bowl
Deep drinks the warrior's soul,
Skoal! to the Northland! *skoal!*"
   Thus the tale ended.
     HENRY WADSWORTH LONGFELLOW.

The Revenge.

A BALLAD OF THE FLEET.

Tennyson's (1807–92) "The *Revenge*" finds a welcome here because it is a favourite with teachers of elocution and their audiences. It teaches us to hold life cheap when the nation's safety is at stake.

AT Flores in the Azores Sir Richard Grenville lay,
And a pinnace, like a flutter'd bird, came flying
   from away:
"Spanish ships of war at sea! we have sighted
   fifty-three!"
Then sware Lord Thomas Howard: "'Fore God,
   I am no coward;
But I cannot meet them here, for my ships are
   out of gear,
And the half my men are sick. I must fly, but
   follow quick.
We are six ships of the line; can we fight with
   fifty-three?"

Then spake Sir Richard Grenville: "I know
  you are no coward;
You fly them for a moment, to fight with them again.
But I've ninety men and more that are lying sick
  ashore.
I should count myself the coward if I left them,
  my Lord Howard,
To these Inquisition dogs and the devildoms of
  Spain."

So Lord Howard passed away with five ships of
  war that day,
Till he melted like a cloud in the silent summer
  heaven;
But Sir Richard bore in hand all his sick men
  from the land
Very carefully and slow,
Men of Bideford in Devon,
And we laid them on the ballast down below;
For we brought them all aboard,
And they blest him in their pain that they were
  not left to Spain,
To the thumbscrew and the stake, for the glory
  of the Lord.

He had only a hundred seamen to work the ship
  and to fight,
And he sail'd away from Flores till the Spaniard
  came in sight,
With his huge sea-castles heaving upon the weather
  bow.
"Shall we fight or shall we fly?
Good Sir Richard, tell us now,
For to fight is but to die!

There'll be little of us left by the time this sun
    be set."
And Sir Richard said again: "We be all good
    Englishmen.
Let us bang these dogs of Seville, the children of
    the devil,
For I never turn'd my back upon Don or devil yet."

Sir Richard spoke and he laugh'd, and we roar'd
    a hurrah, and so
The little *Revenge* ran on sheer into the heart of
    the foe,
With her hundred fighters on deck, and her
    ninety sick below;
For half of their fleet to the right and half to the
    left were seen,
And the little *Revenge* ran on thro' the long sea-
    lane between.

Thousands of their soldiers look'd down from
    their decks and laugh'd,
Thousands of their seamen made mock at the
    mad little craft
Running on and on, till delay'd
By their mountain-like *San Philip* that, of fifteen
    hundred tons,
And up-shadowing high above us with her yawning
    tiers of guns,
Took the breath from our sails, and we stay'd.

And while now the great *San Philip* hung above
    us like a cloud
Whence the thunderbolt will fall
Long and loud,

Four galleons drew away
From the Spanish fleet that day,
And two upon the larboard and two upon the
  starboard lay,
And the battle-thunder broke from them all.

But anon the great *San Philip*, she bethought
  herself and went,
Having that within her womb that had left her
  ill content;
And the rest they came aboard us, and they
  fought us hand to hand,
For a dozen times they came with their pikes and
  musqueteers,
And a dozen times we shook 'em off as a dog
  that shakes his ears
When he leaps from the water to the land.

And the sun went down, and the stars came out
  far over the summer sea,
But never a moment ceased the fight of the one
  and the fifty-three;
Ship after ship, the whole night long, their high-
  built galleons came,
Ship after ship, the whole night long, with her
  battle-thunder and flame;
Ship after ship, the whole night long, drew back
  with her dead and her shame.
For some were sunk and many were shatter'd,
  and so could fight us no more—
God of battles, was ever a battle like this in the
  world before?

For he said, "Fight on! fight on!"
Tho' his vessel was all but a wreck;
And it chanced that, when half of the short
    summer night was gone,
With a grisly wound to be drest he had left the
    deck,
But a bullet struck him that was dressing it
    suddenly dead,
And himself he was wounded again in the side
    and the head,
And he said, "Fight on! Fight on!"

And the night went down, and the sun smiled
    out far over the summer sea,
And the Spanish fleet with broken sides lay
    round us all in a ring;
But they dared not touch us again, for they
    fear'd that we still could sting,
So they watch'd what the end would be.
And we had not fought them in vain,
But in perilous plight were we,
Seeing forty of our poor hundred were slain,
And half of the rest of us maim'd for life
In the crash of the cannonades and the desperate
    strife;
And the sick men down in the hold were most
    of them stark and cold,
And the pikes were all broken or bent, and the
    powder was all of it spent;
And the masts and the rigging were lying over
    the side;
But Sir Richard cried in his English pride:

"We have fought such a fight for a day and a
night
As may never be fought again!
We have won great glory, my men!
And a day less or more
At sea or ashore,
We die—does it matter when?
Sink me the ship, Master Gunner—sink her,
split her in twain!
Fall into the hands of God, not into the hands
of Spain!"

And the gunner said, "Ay, ay," but the seamen
made reply:
"We have children, we have wives,
And the Lord hath spared our lives.
We will make the Spaniard promise, if we yield,
to let us go;
We shall live to fight again, and to strike another
blow."
And the lion there lay dying, and they yielded
to the foe.
And the stately Spanish men to their flagship
bore him then,
Where they laid him by the mast, old Sir Richard
caught at last,
And they praised him to his face with their
courtly foreign grace;
But he rose upon their decks, and he cried:
"I have fought for Queen and Faith like a valiant
man and true;
I have only done my duty as a man is bound to
do.

With a joyful spirit I, Sir Richard Grenville, die !"
And he fell upon their decks, and he died.

And they stared at the dead that had been so
valiant and true,
And had holden the power and glory of Spain so
cheap
That he dared her with one little ship and his
English few.
Was he devil or man? He was devil for aught
they knew,
But they sank his body with honour down into
the deep,
And they mann'd the *Revenge* with a swarthier
alien crew,
And away she sail'd with her loss and long'd
for her own;
When a wind from the lands they had ruin'd
awoke from sleep,
And the water began to heave and the weather
to moan,
And or ever that evening ended a great gale blew,
And a wave like the wave that is raised by an
earthquake grew,
Till it smote on their hulls, and their sails, and
their masts, and their flags,
And the whole sea plunged and fell on the shot-
shatter'd navy of Spain,
And the little *Revenge* herself went down by the
island crags,
To be lost evermore in the main.

ALFRED TENNYSON.

Sir Galahad.

Sir Galahad is the most moral and upright of all the Knights of the Round Table. The strong lines of the poem (Tennyson, 1809-92) are the strong lines of human destiny—

"My strength is as the strength of ten
Because my heart is pure."

My good blade carves the casques of men,
  My tough lance thrusteth sure,
My strength is as the strength of ten,
  Because my heart is pure.
The shattering trumpet shrilleth high,
  The hard brands shiver on the steel,
The splinter'd spear-shafts crack and fly,
  The horse and rider reel:
They reel, they roll in clanging lists,
  And when the tide of combat stands,
Perfume and flowers fall in showers,
  That lightly rain from ladies' hands.

How sweet are looks that ladies bend
  On whom their favours fall!
For them I battle till the end,
  To save from shame and thrall:
But all my heart is drawn above,
  My knees are bow'd in crypt and shrine:
I never felt the kiss of love,
  Nor maiden's hand in mine.
More bounteous aspects on me beam,
  Me mightier transports move and thrill;
So keep I fair thro' faith and prayer
  A virgin heart in work and will.

When down the stormy crescent goes,
   A light before me swims,
Between dark stems the forest glows,
   I hear a noise of hymns:
Then by some secret shrine I ride;
   I hear a voice, but none are there;
The stalls are void, the doors are wide,
   The tapers burning fair.
Fair gleams the snowy altar-cloth,
   The silver vessels sparkle clean,
The shrill bell rings, the censer swings,
   And solemn chaunts resound between.

Sometimes on lonely mountain-meres
   I find a magic bark;
I leap on board: no helmsman steers:
   I float till all is dark.
A gentle sound, an awful light!
   Three angels bear the holy Grail:
With folded feet, in stoles of white,
   On sleeping wings they sail.
Ah, blessèd vision! blood of God!
   My spirit beats her mortal bars,
As down dark tides the glory slides,
   And star-like mingles with the stars.

When on my goodly charger borne
   Thro' dreaming towns I go,
The cock crows ere the Christmas morn,
   The streets are dumb with snow.
The tempest crackles on the leads,
   And, ringing, springs from brand and mail;

But o'er the dark a glory spreads,
    And gilds the driving hail.
I leave the plain, I climb the height;
    No branchy thicket shelter yields;
But blessèd forms in whistling storms
    Fly o'er waste fens and windy fields.

A maiden knight—to me is given
    Such hope, I know not fear;
I yearn to breathe the airs of heaven
    That often meet me here.
I muse on joy that will not cease,
    Pure spaces cloth'd in living beams,
Pure lilies of eternal peace,
    Whose odours haunt my dreams;
And, stricken by an angel's hand,
    This mortal armour that I wear,
This weight and size, this heart and eyes,
    Are touch'd, are turn'd to finest air.

The clouds are broken in the sky,
    And thro' the mountain-walls
A rolling organ-harmony
    Swells up, and shakes and falls.
Then move the trees, the copses nod,
    Wings flutter, voices hover clear:
"O just and faithful knight of God!
    Ride on! the prize is near."
So pass I hostel, hall, and grange;
    By bridge and ford, by park and pale,
All-arm'd I ride, whate'er betide,
    Until I find the holy Grail.

ALFRED TENNYSON.

A Name in the Sand.

"A Name in the Sand," by Hannah Flagg Gould (1789-1865), is a poem to correct our ready overestimate of our own importance.

ALONE I walked the ocean strand;
A pearly shell was in my hand:
I stooped and wrote upon the sand
    My name—the year—the day.
As onward from the spot I passed,
One lingering look behind I cast;
A wave came rolling high and fast,
    And washed my lines away.

And so, methought, 'twill shortly be
With every mark on earth from me:
A wave of dark oblivion's sea
    Will sweep across the place
Where I have trod the sandy shore
Of time, and been, to be no more,
Of me—my day—the name I bore,
    To leave nor track nor trace.

And yet, with Him who counts the sands
And holds the waters in His hands,
I know a lasting record stands
    Inscribed against my name,
Of all this mortal part has wrought,
Of all this thinking soul has thought,
And from these fleeting moments caught
    For glory or for shame.

                HANNAH FLAGG GOULD.

PART VI.

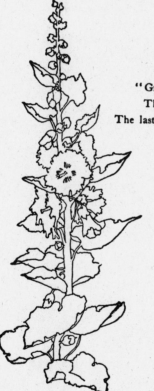

"Grow old along with me!
The best is yet to be,—
The last of life, for which the first
was made."

PART VI.

The Voice of Spring.

"The Voice of Spring," by Felicia Hemans (1749–1835), becomes attractive as years go on. The line in this poem that captivated my youthful fancy was:
"The larch has hung all his tassels forth."
The delight with which trees hang out their new little tassels every year is one of the charms of "the pine family." John Burroughs sent us down a tiny hemlock, that grew in our window-box at school for five years, and every spring it was a new joy on account of the fine, tender tassels. Mrs. Hemans had a vivid imagination backed up by an abundant information.

I COME, I come ! ye have called me long;
I come o'er the mountains, with light and song.
Ye may trace my step o'er the waking earth
By the winds which tell of the violet's birth,
By the primrose stars in the shadowy grass,
By the green leaves opening as I pass.

I have breathed on the South, and the chestnut-
flowers
By thousands have burst from the forest bowers,
And the ancient graves and the fallen fanes
Are veiled with wreaths on Italian plains;
But it is not for me, in my hour of bloom,
To speak of the ruin or the tomb !

I have looked o'er the hills of the stormy North,
And the larch has hung all his tassels forth;
The fisher is out on the sunny sea,
And the reindeer bounds o'er the pastures free,
And the pine has a fringe of softer green,
And the moss looks bright, where my step has been.

I have sent through the wood-paths a glowing sigh,
And called out each voice of the deep blue sky,
From the night-bird's lay through the starry time,
In the groves of the soft Hesperian clime,
To the swan's wild note by the Iceland lakes,
When the dark fir-branch into verdure breaks.

From the streams and founts I have loosed the
    chain;
They are sweeping on to the silvery main,
They are flashing down from the mountain brows,
They are flinging spray o'er the forest boughs,
They are bursting fresh from their sparry caves,
And the earth resounds with the joy of waves.

                    FELICIA HEMANS.

The Forsaken Merman.

"The Forsaken Merman," by Matthew Arnold (1822–88), is a poem
that I do not expect children to appreciate fully, even when they care
enough for it to learn it. It is too long for most children to commit
to memory, and I generally assign one stanza to one pupil and another
to another pupil until it is divided up among them. The poem is a
masterpiece. Doubtless the poet meant to show that the forsaken
merman had a greater soul to save than the woman who sought to save
her soul by deserting natural duty. Salvation does not come through
the faith that builds itself at the expense of love.

COME, dear children, let us away;
Down and away below!
Now my brothers call from the bay,
Now the great winds shoreward blow,
Now the salt tides seaward flow;
Now the wild white horses play,
Champ and chafe and toss in the spray.
Children dear, let us away!
This way, this way!

Call her once before you go—
Call once yet !
In a voice that she will know:
"Margaret ! Margaret !"
Children's voices should be dear
(Call once more) to a mother's ear;
Children's voices, wild with pain--
Surely she will come again !
Call her once and come away;
This way, this way !
"Mother dear, we cannot stay !
The wild white horses foam and fret."
Margaret ! Margaret !

Come, dear children, come away down;
Call no more !
One last look at the white-wall'd town,
And the little gray church on the windy shore;
Then come down !
She will not come though you call all day;
Come away, come away !

Children dear, was it yesterday
We heard the sweet bells over the bay ?
In the caverns where we lay,
Through the surf and through the swell,
The far-off sound of a silver bell ?
Sand-strewn caverns, cool and deep.
Where the winds are all asleep;
Where the spent lights quiver and gleam,
Where the salt weed sways in the stream,
Where the sea-beasts, ranged all round,
Feed in the ooze of their pasture-ground;

Where the sea-snakes coil and twine,
Dry their mail and bask in the brine;
Where great whales come sailing by,
Sail and sail, with unshut eye,
Round the world forever and aye?
When did music come this way?
Children dear, was it yesterday?

Children dear, was it yesterday
(Call yet once) that she went away?
Once she sate with you and me,
On a red gold throne in the heart of the sea,
And the youngest sate on her knee.
She comb'd its bright hair, and she tended it well,
When down swung the sound of a far-off bell.
She sigh'd, she look'd up through the clear green
    sea;
She said: "I must go, for my kinsfolk pray
In the little gray church on the shore to-day.
'Twill be Easter-time in the world—ah me!
And I lose my poor soul, Merman! here with thee."
I said: "Go up, dear heart, through the waves;
Say thy prayer, and come back to the kind sea-
    caves!"
She smil'd, she went up through the surf in the bay.

Children dear, was it yesterday?
Children dear, were we long alone?
"The sea grows·stormy, the little ones moan;
Long prayers," I said, "in the world they say;
Come!" I said; and we rose through the surf in
    the bay.

We went up the beach, by the sandy down
Where the sea-stocks bloom, to the white-wall'd
  town;
Through the narrow pav'd streets, where all was
  still,
To the little gray church on the windy hill.
From the church came a murmur of folk at their
  prayers,
But we stood without in the cold blowing airs.
We climb'd on the graves, on the stones worn with
  rains,
And we gaz'd up the aisle through the small leaded
  panes.
She sate by the pillar; we saw her clear:
"Margaret, hist! come quick, we are here!
Dear heart," I said, "we are long alone;
The sea grows stormy, the little ones moan."
But, ah, she gave me never a look,
For her eyes were seal'd to the holy book!
Loud prays the priest: shut stands the door.
Come away, children, call no more!
Come away, come down, call no more!

Down, down, down!
Down to the depths of the sea!
She sits at her wheel in the humming town,
Singing most joyfully.
Hark what she sings: "O joy, O joy,
For the humming street, and the child with its toy!
For the priest, and the bell, and the holy well;
For the wheel where I spun,
And the blessèd light of the sun!"
And so she sings her fill,

Singing most joyfully,
Till the spindle drops from her hand,
And the whizzing wheel stands still.
She steals to the window, and looks at the sand,
And over the sand at the sea;
And her eyes are set in a stare;
And anon there breaks a sigh,
And anon there drops a tear,
From a sorrow-clouded eye,
And a heart sorrow-laden,
A long, long sigh;
For the cold strange eyes of a little Mermaiden
And the gleam of her golden hair.

Come away, away, children;
Come, children, come down!
The hoarse wind blows colder;
Lights shine in the town.
She will start from her slumber
When gusts shake the door;
She will hear the winds howling,
Will hear the waves roar.
We shall see, while above us
The waves roar and whirl,
A ceiling of amber,
A pavement of pearl.
Singing: "Here came a mortal,
But faithless was she!
And alone dwell forever
The kings of the sea."

But, children, at midnight,
When soft the winds blow,

When clear falls the moonlight,
When spring-tides are low;
When sweet airs come seaward
From heaths starr'd with broom,
And high rocks throw mildly
On the blanch'd sands a gloom;
Up the still, glistening beaches,
Up the creeks we will hie,
Over banks of bright seaweed
The ebb-tide leaves dry.
We will gaze, from the sand-hills,
At the white, sleeping town;
At the church on the hill-side—
And then come back down.
Singing: "There dwells a lov'd one,
But cruel is she!
She left lonely forever
The kings of the sea."

MATTHEW ARNOLD.

The Banks o' Doon.

"The Banks o' Doon," by Robert Burns (1759–96). Bonnie
Doon is in the southwestern part of Scotland. Robert Burns's old
home is close to it. The house has low walls, a thatched roof, and
only two rooms. Alloway Kirk and the two bridges so famous in
Robert Burns's verse are near by. This is an enchanted land, and
the Scotch people for miles around Ayr speak of the poet with sincere
affection. Burns, more than any other poet, has thrown the enchant-
ment of poetry over his own locality.

YE banks and braes o' bonnie Doon,
    How can ye blume sae fair!
How can ye chant, ye little birds,
    And I sae fu' o' care.

Thou'lt break my heart, thou bonnie bird
   That sings upon the bough;
Thou minds me o' the happy days
   When my fause luve was true.

Thou'lt break my heart, thou bonnie bird
   That sings beside thy mate;
For sae I sat, and sae I sang,
   And wist na o' my fate.

Aft hae I rov'd by bonnie Doon,
   To see the woodbine twine,
And ilka bird sang o' its love,
   And sae did I o' mine.

Wi' lightsome heart I pu'd a rose
   Frae off its thorny tree;
And my fause luver staw the rose,
   But left the thorn wi' me.

ROBERT BURNS.

The Light of Other Days.

OFT in the stilly night
   Ere slumber's chain has bound me,
Fond Memory brings the light
   Of other days around me:
     The smiles, the tears
     Of boyhood's years,
   The words of love then spoken;
     The eyes that shone,
     Now dimmed and gone,
   The cheerful hearts now broken!
Thus in the stilly night
   Ere slumber's chain has bound me,

Sad Memory brings the light
 Of other days around me.

When I remember all
  The friends so link'd together
I've seen around me fall
  Like leaves in wintry weather,
    I feel like one
    Who treads alone
  Some banquet-hall deserted,
    Whose lights are fled,
    Whose garlands dead,
  And all but he departed!
Thus in the stilly night
  Ere slumber's chain has bound me,
Sad Memory brings the light
  Of other days around me.

THOMAS MOORE.

My Own Shall Come to Me.

If John Burroughs (1837–) had never written any other poem
than "My Own Shall Come to Me," he would have stood to all ages as
one of the greatest of American poets. The poem is most character-
istic of the tall, majestic, slow-going poet and naturalist. There is
no greater line in Greek or English literature than

"I stand amid the eternal ways."

SERENE I fold my hands and wait,
  Nor care for wind, nor tide, nor sea.
I rave no more 'gainst time or fate,
  For lo! my own shall come to me.

I stay my haste, I make delays,
  For what avails this eager pace?
I stand amid the eternal ways,
  And what is mine shall know my face.

Asleep, awake, by night or day
    The friends I seek are seeking me;
No wind can drive my bark astray,
    Nor change the tide of destiny.

What matter if I stand alone?
    I wait with joy the coming years;
My heart shall reap when it has sown,
    And gather up its fruit of tears.

The stars come nightly to the sky;
    The tidal wave comes to the sea;
Nor time, nor space, nor deep, nor high,
    Can keep my own away from me.

The waters know their own and draw
    The brook that springs in yonder heights;
So flows the good with equal law
    Unto the soul of pure delights.

                JOHN BURROUGHS.

Ode to a Skylark.

"Ode to a Skylark," by Percy Bysshe Shelley (1792–1822), is usually assigned to "grammar grades" of schools. It is included here out of respect to a boy of eleven years who was more impressed with these lines than with any other lines in any poem:
        "Like a poet hidden,
           In the light of thought
        Singing songs unbidden
           Till the world is wrought
To sympathy with hopes and fears it heeded not."

HAIL to thee, blithe spirit—
    Bird thou never wert—
That from heaven or near it
    Pourest thy full heart
In profuse strains of unpremeditated art.

Higher still and higher
   From the earth thou springest,
Like a cloud of fire;
   The blue deep thou wingest,
And singing still dost soar and soaring ever singest.

In the golden lightning
   Of the sunken sun,
O'er which clouds are bright'ning,
   Thou dost float and run,
Like an unbodied joy whose race is just begun.

The pale purple even
   Melts around thy flight;
Like a star of heaven,
   In the broad daylight
Thou art unseen, but yet I hear thy shrill delight.

All the earth and air
   With thy voice is loud,
As, when night is bare,
   From one lonely cloud
The moon rains out her beams, and heaven is
     overflowed.

What thou art we know not;
   What is most like thee?
From rainbow-clouds there flow not
   Drops so bright to see
As from thy presence showers a rain of melody:—

Like a poet hidden
   In the light of thought;

Singing hymns unbidden,
   Till the world is wrought
To sympathy with hopes and fears it heeded not.

Teach us, sprite or bird,
   What sweet thoughts are thine:
I have never heard
   Praise of love or wine
That panted forth a flood of rapture so divine.

Chorus hymeneal
   Or triumphal chaunt,
Matched with thine, would be all
   But an empty vaunt—
A thing wherein we feel there is some hidden want.

What objects are the fountains
   Of thy happy strain?
What fields, or waves, or mountains?
   What shapes of sky or plain?
What love of thine own kind? what ignorance of
   pain?

Teach me half the gladness
   That thy brain must know,
Such harmonious madness
   From my lips would flow,
The world should listen then, as I am listening
   now!

PERCY BYSSHE SHELLEY.

The Sands of Dee.

I have often had the pleasure of riding across the coast from Chester, England, to Rhyl, on the north coast of Wales, where stretch "The Sands of Dee" (Charles Kingsley, 1819–75). These purple sands at low tide stretch off into the sea miles away, and are said to be full of quicksands.

"O MARY, go and call the cattle home,
  And call the cattle home,
  And call the cattle home,
 Across the sands of Dee."
The western wind was wild and dark with foam
 And all alone went she.

The western tide crept up along the sand,
  And o'er and o'er the sand,
  And round and round the sand,
 As far as eye could see.
The rolling mist came down and hid the land;
 And never home came she.

Oh! is it weed, or fish, or floating hair,—
  A tress of golden hair,
  A drownèd maiden's hair,
 Above the nets at sea?
Was never salmon yet that shone so fair
 Among the stakes on Dee.

They rowed her in across the rolling foam,
  The cruel crawling foam,
  The cruel hungry foam,
 To her grave beside the sea.
But still the boatmen hear her call the cattle home
 Across the sands of Dee.
      CHARLES KINGSLEY.

A Wish.

"A Wish" (by Samuel Rogers, 1763-1855) and "Lucy" (by Words-
worth, 1770-1850) are two gems that can be valued only for the spirit
of quiet and modesty diffused by them.

MINE be a cot beside the hill;
    A bee-hive's hum shall soothe my ear;
A willowy brook that turns a mill
    With many a fall shall linger near.

The swallow, oft, beneath my thatch
    Shall twitter from her clay-built nest;
Oft shall the pilgrim lift the latch,
    And share my meal, a welcome guest.

Around my ivied porch shall spring
    Each fragrant flower that drinks the dew;
And Lucy, at her wheel, shall sing
    In russet gown and apron blue.

The village church among the trees,
    Where first our marriage-vows were given,
With merry peals shall swell the breeze
    And point with taper spire to Heaven.
                S. ROGERS.

Lucy.

SHE dwelt among the untrodden ways
    Beside the springs of Dove;
A maid whom there were none to praise,
    And very few to love.

A violet by a mossy stone
   Half-hidden from the eye!
Fair as a star, when only one
   Is shining in the sky.

She lived unknown, and few could know
   When Lucy ceased to be;
But she is in her grave, and, oh,
   The difference to me!

              WILLIAM WORDSWORTH.

Solitude.

HAPPY the man, whose wish and care
A few paternal acres bound,
Content to breathe his native air
          In his own ground.

Whose herds with milk, whose fields with
   bread,
Whose flocks supply him with attire;
Whose trees in summer yield him shade,
          In winter fire.

Blest, who can unconcern'dly find
Hours, days, and years slide soft away
In health of body, peace of mind,
          Quiet by day,

Sound sleep by night; study and ease
Together mixt, sweet recreation,
And innocence, which most does please
          With meditation.

Thus let me live, unseen, unknown;
Thus unlamented let me die;
Steal from the world, and not a stone
      Tell where I lie.
          ALEXANDER POPE.

John Anderson.

"John Anderson," by Robert Burns (1759-96). This poem is
included to please several teachers.

JOHN ANDERSON, my jo, John,
When we were first acquent
Your locks were like the raven,
Your bonnie brow was brent;
But now your brow is bald, John,
Your locks are like the snow;
But blessings on your frosty pow,
John Anderson, my jo.

John Anderson, my jo, John,
We clamb the hill thegither,
And mony a canty day, John,
We've had wi' ane anither;
Now we maun totter down, John,
But hand in hand we'll go,
And sleep thegither at the foot,
John Anderson, my jo.
          ROBERT BURNS.

The God of Music.

"The God of Music," by Edith M. Thomas, an Ohio poetess now living. In this sonnet the poetess has touched the power of Wordsworth or Keats and placed herself among the immortals.

THE God of Music dwelleth out of doors.
All seasons through his minstrelsy we meet,
Breathing by field and covert haunting-sweet
From organ-lofts in forests old he pours:
A solemn harmony: on leafy floors
To smooth autumnal pipes he moves his feet,
Or with the tingling plectrum of the sleet
In winter keen beats out his thrilling scores.
Leave me the reed unplucked beside the stream,
And he will stoop and fill it with the breeze;
Leave me the viol's frame in secret trees,
Unwrought, and it shall wake a druid theme;
Leave me the whispering shell on Nereid shores.
The God of Music dwelleth out of doors.

EDITH M. THOMAS.

A Musical Instrument.

"A Musical Instrument" (by Elizabeth Barrett Browning (1806–61). This poem is the supreme masterpiece of Mrs. Browning. The prime thought in it is the sacrifice and pain that must go to make a poet or any genius.

"The great god sighed for the cost and the pain."

WHAT was he doing, the great god Pan,
   Down in the reeds by the river?
Spreading ruin and scattering ban,
Splashing and paddling with hoofs of a goat,
And breaking the golden lilies afloat
   With the dragon-fly on the river.

He tore out a reed, the great god Pan,
From the deep cool bed of the river:
The limpid water turbidly ran,
And the broken lilies a-dying lay,
And the dragon-fly had fled away,
Ere he brought it out of the river.

High on the shore sat the great god Pan,
While turbidly flow'd the river;
And hack'd and hew'd as a great god can,
With his hard bleak steel at the patient reed,
Till there was not a sign of a leaf indeed
To prove it fresh from the river.

He cut it short, did the great god Pan
(How tall it stood in the river!),
Then drew the pith, like the heart of a man,
Steadily from the outside ring,
And notch'd the poor dry empty thing
In holes, as he sat by the river.

"This is the way," laugh'd the great god Pan
(Laugh'd while he sat by the river),
"The only way, since gods began
To make sweet music, they could succeed."
Then, dropping his mouth to a hole in the reed,
He blew in power by the river.

Sweet, sweet, sweet, O Pan!
Piercing sweet by the river!
Blinding sweet, O great god Pan!
The sun on the hill forgot to die,
And the lilies reviv'd, and the dragon-fly
Came back to dream on the river.

Yet half a beast is the great god Pan,
   To laugh as he sits by the river,
Making a poet out of a man:
The true gods sigh for the cost and pain,—
For the reed which grows nevermore again
   As a reed with the reeds in the river.

ELIZABETH BARRETT BROWNING.

The Brides of Enderby.

"The Brides of Enderby," by Jean Ingelow (1830–97). This poem is very dramatic, and the music of the refrain has done much to make it popular. But the pathos is that which endears it.

THE old mayor climb'd the belfry tower,
   The ringers ran by two, by three;
"Pull, if ye never pull'd before;
   Good ringers, pull your best," quoth he.
"Play uppe, play uppe, O Boston bells!
Ply all your changes, all your swells,
   Play uppe, 'The Brides of Enderby.'"

Men say it was a stolen tyde—
   The Lord that sent it, He knows all;
But in myne ears doth still abide
   The message that the bells let fall:
And there was naught of strange, beside
The flight of mews and peewits pied
   By millions crouch'd on the old sea wall.

I sat and spun within the doore,
   My thread brake off, I rais'd myne eyes;
The level sun, like ruddy ore,
   Lay sinking in the barren skies:

And dark against day's golden death
She moved where Lindis wandereth,
My sonne's faire wife, Elizabeth.

"Cusha! Cusha! Cusha!" calling,
Ere the early dews were falling,
Farre away I heard her song,
"Cusha! Cusha!" all along;
Where the reedy Lindis floweth,
     Floweth, floweth,
From the meads where melick groweth
Faintly came her milking song—

"Cusha! Cusha! Cusha!" calling,
"For the dews will soone be falling;
Leave your meadow grasses mellow,
     Mellow, mellow;
Quit your cowslips, cowslips yellow;
Come uppe, Whitefoot, come uppe, Lightfoot;
Quit the stalks of parsley hollow,
     Hollow, hollow;
Come uppe, Jetty, rise and follow,
From the clovers lift your head;
Come uppe, Whitefoot, come uppe, Lightfoot,
Come uppe, Jetty, rise and follow,
Jetty, to the milking shed."

If it be long, ay, long ago,
    When I beginne to think howe long,
Againe I hear the Lindis flow,
    Swift as an arrowe, sharpe and strong;
And all the aire, it seemeth mee,
Bin full of floating bells (sayth shee),
That ring the tune of Enderby.

Alle fresh the level pasture lay,
  And not a shadowe mote be seene,
Save where full fyve good miles away
  The steeple tower'd from out the greene;
And lo! the great bell farre and wide
Was heard in all the country side
That Saturday at eventide.

The swanherds where their sedges are
  Mov'd on in sunset's golden breath,
The shepherde lads I heard afarre,
  And my sonne's wife, Elizabeth;
Till floating o'er the grassy sea
Came downe that kyndly message free,
The "Brides of Mavis Enderby."

Then some look'd uppe into the sky,
  And all along where Lindis flows
To where the goodly vessels lie,
  And where the lordly steeple shows.
They sayde, "And why should this thing be?
What danger lowers by land or sea?
They ring the tune of Enderby!

"For evil news from Mablethorpe,
  Of pyrate galleys warping down;
For shippes ashore beyond the scorpe,
  They have not spar'd to wake the towne:
But while the west bin red to see,
And storms be none, and pyrates flee,
Why ring 'The Brides of Enderby'?"

I look'd without, and lo! my sonne
  Came riding downe with might and main:

He rais'd a shout as he drew on,
   Till all the welkin rang again,
"Elizabeth! Elizabeth!"
(A sweeter woman ne'er drew breath
Than my sonne's wife, Elizabeth.)

"The olde sea wall," he cried, "is downe,
   The rising tide comes on apace,
And boats adrift in yonder towne
   Go sailing uppe the market-place."
He shook as one that looks on death:
"God save you, mother!" straight he saith;
"Where is my wife, Elizabeth?"

"Good sonne, where Lindis winds her way,
   With her two bairns I marked her long;
And ere yon bells beganne to play
   Afar I heard her milking song."
He looked across the grassy lea,
To right, to left, "Ho, Enderby!"
They rang "The Brides of Enderby!"

With that he cried and beat his breast;
   For, lo! along the river's bed
A mighty eygre rear'd his crest,
   And uppe the Lindis raging sped.
It swept with thunderous noises loud;
Shap'd like a curling snow-white cloud,
Or like a demon in a shroud.

And rearing Lindis backward press'd
   Shook all her trembling bankes amaine;
Then madly at the eygre's breast
   Flung uppe her weltering walls again.

Then bankes came downe with ruin and rout—
Then beaten foam flew round about—
Then all the mighty floods were out.

So farre, so fast the eygre drave,
    The heart had hardly time to beat
Before a shallow seething wave
    Sobb'd in the grasses at oure feet:
The feet had hardly time to flee
Before it brake against the knee,
And all the world was in the sea.

Upon the roofe we sate that night,
    The noise of bells went sweeping by;
I mark'd the lofty beacon light
    Stream from the church tower, red and
        high—
A lurid mark and dread to see;
And awsome bells they were to mee,
That in the dark rang "Enderby."

They rang the sailor lads to guide
    From roofe to roofe who fearless row'd;
And I—my sonne was at my side,
    And yet the ruddy beacon glow'd:
And yet he moan'd beneath his breath,
"O come in life, or come in death!
O lost! my love, Elizabeth."

And didst thou visit him no more?
    Thou didst, thou didst, my daughter deare
The waters laid thee at his doore,
    Ere yet the early dawn was clear.

Thy pretty bairns in fast embrace,
The lifted sun shone on thy face,
Downe drifted to thy dwelling-place.

That flow strew'd wrecks about the grass,
     That ebbe swept out the flocks to sea;
A fatal ebbe and flow, alas!
     To manye more than myne and mee;
But each will mourn his own (she saith);
And sweeter woman ne'er drew breath
Than my sonne's wife, Elizabeth.

I shall never hear her more
By the reedy Lindis shore,
"Cusha! Cusha! Cusha!" calling,
Ere the early dews be falling;
I shall never hear her song,
"Cusha! Cusha!" all along
Where the sunny Lindis floweth,
     Goeth, floweth;
From the meads where melick groweth,
     When the water winding down,
     Onward floweth to the town.

I shall never see her more
Where the reeds and rushes quiver,
     Shiver, quiver;
Stand beside the sobbing river,
Sobbing, throbbing, in its falling
To the sandy lonesome shore;
I shall never hear her calling,
"Leave your meadow grasses mellow,
     Mellow, mellow;
Quit your cowslips, cowslips yellow;

Come uppe, Whitefoot, come uppe, Lightfoot;
Quit your pipes of parsley hollow,
    Hollow, hollow;
Come uppe, Lightfoot, rise and follow;
    Lightfoot, Whitefoot,
From your clovers lift the head;
Come uppe, Jetty, follow, follow,
Jetty, to the milking shed."

                  JEAN INGELOW.

The Lye.

"The Lye," by Sir Walter Raleigh (1552–1618), is one of the strongest and most appealing poems a teacher can read to her pupils when teaching early American history. The poem is full of magnificent lines, such as "Go, soul, the body's guest." The poem never lacks an attentive audience of young people when correlated with the study of North Carolina and Sir Walter Raleigh. The solitary, majestic character of Sir Walter Raleigh, his intrepidity while undergoing tortures inflicted by a cowardly king, the ring of indignation—all these make a weapon for him stronger than the ax that beheaded him. In this poem he "has the last word."

GOE, soule, the bodie's guest,
    Upon a thanklesse arrant;
Feare not to touche the best—
    The truth shall be thy warrant!
      Goe, since I needs must dye,
      And give the world the lye.

Goe tell the court it glowes
    And shines like rotten wood;
Goe tell the church it showes
    What's good, and doth no good;
      If church and court reply,
      Then give them both the lye.

Tell potentates they live
   Acting by others' actions—
Not loved unlesse they give,
   Not strong but by their factions;
     If potentates reply,
     Give potentates the lye.

Tell men of high condition,
   That rule affairs of state,
Their purpose is ambition,
   Their practice only hate;
     And if they once reply,
     Then give them all the lye.

Tell zeale it lacks devotion;
   Tell love it is but lust;
Tell time it is but motion;
   Tell flesh it is but dust;
     And wish them not reply,
     For thou must give the lye.

Tell wit how much it wrangles
   In tickle points of nicenesse;
Tell wisdome she entangles
   Herselfe in over-wisenesse;
     And if they do reply,
     Straight give them both the lye.

Tell physicke of her boldnesse;
   Tell skill it is pretension;
Tell charity of coldnesse;
   Tell law it is contention;
     And as they yield reply,
     So give them still the lye.

Tell fortune of her blindnesse;
  Tell nature of decay;
Tell friendship of unkindnesse;
  Tell justice of delay;
    And if they dare reply,
    Then give them all the lye.

Tell arts they have no soundnesse,
  But vary by esteeming;
Tell schooles they want profoundnesse,
  And stand too much on seeming;
    If arts and schooles reply,
    Give arts and schooles the lye.

So, when thou hast, as I
  Commanded thee, done blabbing—
Although to give the lye
  Deserves no less than stabbing—
    Yet stab at thee who will,
    No stab the soule can kill.

SIR WALTER RALEIGH.

L'Envoi.

"L'Envoi," by Rudyard Kipling, is a favourite on account of its sweeping assertion of the individual's right to self-development.

WHEN Earth's last picture is painted, and the
  tubes are twisted and dried,
When the oldest colours have faded, and the
  youngest critic has died,
We shall rest, and, faith, we shall need it—lie
  down for an æon or two,
Till the Master of All Good Workmen shall set us
  to work anew!

And those who were good shall be happy: they
    shall sit in a golden chair;
They shall splash at a ten-league canvas with
    brushes of comet's hair;
They shall find real saints to draw from—Magda-
    lene, Peter, and Paul;
They shall work for an age at a sitting and never
    be tired at all!

And only the Master shall praise us, and only
    the Master shall blame;
And no one shall work for money, and no one
    shall work for fame;
But each for the joy of the working, and each,
    in his separate star,
Shall draw the Thing as he sees It for the God of
    Things as They Are!

                    RUDYARD KIPLING.

Contentment.

"Contentment," by Edward Dyer (1545–1607). This poem holds
much to comfort and control people who are shut up to the joys of
meditation—people to whom the world of activity is closed. To be
independent of things material—this is the soul's pleasure.

My mind to me a kingdom is;
    Such perfect joy therein I find
As far excels all earthly bliss
    That God or Nature hath assigned;
Though much I want that most would have,
Yet still my mind forbids to crave.

Content I live; this is my stay,—
    I seek no more than may suffice.

I press to bear no haughty sway;
   Look, what I lack my mind supplies.
Lo, thus I triumph like a king,
Content with that my mind doth bring.

I laugh not at another's loss,
   I grudge not at another's gain;
No worldly wave my mind can toss;
   I brook that is another's bane.
I fear no foe, nor fawn on friend;
I loathe not life, nor dread mine end.

My wealth is health and perfect ease;
   My conscience clear my chief defense;
I never seek by bribes to please
   Nor by desert to give offense.
Thus do I live, thus will I die;
Would all did so as well as I!

                                  EDWARD DYER.

The Harp That Once Through Tara's Halls.

THE harp that once through Tara's halls
   The soul of music shed,
Now hangs as mute on Tara's walls
   As if that soul were fled.
So sleeps the pride of former days,
   So glory's thrill is o'er,
And hearts, that once beat high for praise,
   Now feel that pulse no more.

No more to chiefs and ladies bright
   The harp of Tara swells:

The chord alone, that breaks at night,
   Its tale of ruin tells.
Thus Freedom now so seldom wakes,
   The only throb she gives
Is when some heart indignant breaks,
   To show that still she lives.

                THOMAS MOORE.

The Old Oaken Bucket.

"The Old Oaken Bucket," by Samuel Woodworth (1785–1848), is a poem we love because it is an elegant expression of something very dear and homely.

How dear to this heart are the scenes of my child-
      hood,
   When fond recollection presents them to view!
The orchard, the meadow, the deep-tangled wild-
      wood,
   And every loved spot which my infancy knew!
The wide-spreading pond, and the mill that stood
      by it,
   The bridge, and the rock where the cataract fell,
The cot of my father, the dairy-house nigh it,
   And e'en the rude bucket that hung in the well—
The old oaken bucket, the iron-bound bucket,
The moss-covered bucket which hung in the well.

That moss-covered vessel I hailed as a treasure,
   For often at noon, when returned from the field,
I found it the source of an exquisite pleasure,
   The purest and sweetest that nature can yield.
How ardent I seized it, with hands that were
      glowing,
   And quick to the white-pebbled bottom it fell;

Then soon, with the emblem of truth overflowing,
 And dripping with coolness, it rose from the
  well—
The old oaken bucket, the iron-bound bucket,
The moss-covered bucket arose from the well.

How sweet from the green mossy brim to receive it,
 As poised on the curb it inclined to my lips!
Not a full blushing goblet could tempt me to leave
 it,
 The brightest that beauty or revelry sips.
And now, far removed from the loved habitation,
 The tear of regret will intrusively swell,
As fancy reverts to my father's plantation,
 And sighs for the bucket that hangs in the well—
The old oaken bucket, the iron-bound bucket,
The moss-covered bucket that hangs in the well!
        SAMUEL WOODWORTH.

The Raven.

"The Raven," by Edgar Allan Poe (1809-49), is placed here
because so many college men speak of it at once as the great poem of
their boyhood. The poem caught me when a child by its refrain and
weird picturesqueness. It has never outgrown its mechanical charm.

ONCE upon a midnight dreary, while I pondered,
 weak and weary,
Over many a quaint and curious volume of for-
 gotten lore—
While I nodded, nearly napping, suddenly there
 came a tapping,
As of some one gently rapping, rapping at my
 chamber door—

"'Tis some visitor," I muttered, "tapping at my
    chamber door—
        Only this, and nothing more."

Ah! distinctly I remember, it was in the bleak
    December,
And each separate dying ember wrought its ghost
    upon the floor;
Eagerly I wished the morrow; vainly I had sought
    to borrow
From my books surcease of sorrow—sorrow for the
    lost Lenore—
For the rare and radiant maiden whom the angels
    name Lenore—
        Nameless here for evermore.

And the silken, sad, uncertain rustling of each
    purple curtain
Thrilled me—filled me with fantastic terrors never
    felt before;
So that now, to still the beating of my heart, I
    stood repeating,
"'Tis some visitor entreating entrance at my
    chamber door—
Some late visitor entreating entrance at my cham-
    ber door:
        This it is, and nothing more."

Presently my soul grew stronger; hesitating then
    no longer,
"Sir," said I, "or madam, truly your forgiveness
    I implore;

But the fact is, I was napping, and so gently you
  came rapping,
And so faintly you came tapping, tapping at my
  chamber door,
That I scarce was sure I heard you." Here I
  opened wide the door:
    Darkness there, and nothing more.

Deep into that darkness peering, long I stood there,
  wondering, fearing,
Doubting, dreaming dreams no mortal ever dared
  to dream before;
But the silence was unbroken, and the stillness
  gave no token,
And the only word there spoken was the whispered
  word, "Lenore!"
This I whispered, and an echo murmured back the
  word, "Lenore!"
    Merely this, and nothing more.

Back into my chamber turning, all my soul within
  me burning,
Soon again I heard a rapping, something louder
  than before:
"Surely," said I, "surely that is something at my
  window lattice;
Let me see, then, what thereat is, and this mystery
  explore—
Let my heart be still a moment, and this mystery
  explore.
    'Tis the wind, and nothing more."

Open here I flung the shutter, when, with many a
    flirt and flutter,
In there stepped a stately Raven, of the saintly
    days of yore;
Not the least obeisance made he, not a minute
    stopped or stayed he;
But with mien of lord or lady, perched above my
    chamber door—
Perched above a bust of Pallas, just above my
    chamber door—
       Perched, and sat, and nothing more.

Then this ebony bird beguiling my sad fancy into
    smiling,
By the grave and stern decorum of the countenance
    it wore;
"Though thy crest be shorn and shaven, thou,"
    I said, "art sure, no craven;
Ghastly, grim, and ancient Raven, wandering
    from the nightly shore,
Tell me what thy lordly name is on the night's
    Plutonian shore?"
       Quoth the Raven, "Nevermore."

Much I marvelled this ungainly fowl to hear dis-
    course so plainly,
Though its answer, little meaning, little relevancy
    bore;
For we cannot help agreeing that no living human
    being
Ever yet was blessed with seeing bird above his
    chamber door—

Bird or beast upon the sculptured bust above his
    chamber door
        With such a name as "Nevermore."

But the Raven, sitting lonely on that placid bust,
    spoke only
That one word, as if his soul in that one word he
    did outpour;
Nothing further then he uttered, not a feather
    then he fluttered,
Till I scarcely more than muttered—"Other
    friends have flown before,
On the morrow he will leave me, as my hopes have
    flown before."
        Then the bird said, "Nevermore."

Startled by the stillness broken by reply so aptly
    spoken,
"Doubtless," said I, "what it utters is its only
    stock and store,
Caught from some unhappy master, whom un-
    merciful disaster
Followed fast and followed faster, till his songs one
    burden bore—
Till the dirges of his hope this melancholy burden
    bore—
        Of 'Never, nevermore.'"

But the Raven still beguiling all my sad soul into
    smiling,
Straight I wheeled a cushioned seat in front of
    bird, and bust, and door;

Then upon the velvet sinking, I betook myself to
    linking
Fancy into fancy, thinking what this ominous bird
    of yore—
What this grim, ungainly, ghastly, gaunt, and
    ominous bird of yore
        Meant in croaking "Nevermore."

Thus I sat engaged in guessing, but no syllable
    expressing
To the fowl whose fiery eyes now burned into my
    bosom's core;
This and more I sat divining, with my head at
    ease reclining
On the cushion's velvet lining, that the lamp-light
    gloated o'er,
But whose velvet violet lining, with the lamp-light
    gloating o'er,
        She shall press, ah, nevermore!

Then methought the air grew denser, perfumed
    from an unseen censer
Swung by seraphim, whose footfalls twinkled on
    the tufted floor.
"Wretch," I cried, "thy God hath lent thee—by
    these angels He hath sent thee
Respite—respite and nepenthe from my memories
    of Lenore!
Quaff, oh, quaff this kind nepenthe, and forget this
    lost Lenore!"
        Quoth the Raven, "Nevermore."

"Prophet," said I, "thing of evil—prophet still,
    if bird or devil!
Whether tempter sent, or whether tempest tossed
    thee here ashore
Desolate, yet all undaunted, on this desert land
    enchanted,
On this home by horror haunted—tell me truly,
    I implore,
Is there—*is* there balm in Gilead?—tell me, tell
    me, I implore!"
        Quoth the Raven, "Nevermore."

"Prophet," said I, "thing of evil!—prophet still,
    if bird or devil!
By that heaven that bends above us—by that God
    we both adore—
Tell this soul, with sorrow laden, if, within the
    distant Aiden
It shall clasp a sainted maiden, whom the angels
    name Lenore!
Clasp a rare and radiant maiden, whom the angels
    name Lenore?"
        Quoth the Raven, "Nevermore."

"Be that our sign of parting, bird or fiend," I
    shrieked, upstarting—
"Get thee back into the tempest and the night's
    Plutonian shore;
Leave no black plume as a token of that lie thy
    soul hath spoken,
Leave my loneliness unbroken—quit the bust
    above my door,

Take thy beak from out my heart and take thy
   form from off my door!"
         Quoth the Raven, "Nevermore."

And the Raven, never flitting, still is sitting, still
   is sitting,
On the pallid bust of Pallas, just above my cham-
   ber door;
And his eyes have all the seeming of a demon's that
   is dreaming,
And the lamp-light o'er him streaming, throws his
   shadow on the floor;
And my soul from out that shadow, that lies float-
   ing on the floor,
         Shall be lifted—nevermore!
                  EDGAR ALLAN POE.

Arnold von Winkleried.

"MAKE way for liberty!" he cried,
Made way for liberty, and died.
In arms the Austrian phalanx stood,
A living wall, a human wood,—
A wall, where every conscious stone
Seemed to its kindred thousands grown.
A rampart all assaults to bear,
Till time to dust their frames should wear:
So still, so dense the Austrians stood,
A living wall, a human wood.

Impregnable their front appears,
All horrent with projected spears,

Whose polished points before them shine,
From flank to flank, one brilliant line,
Bright as the breakers' splendours run
Along the billows to the sun.

Opposed to these a hovering band
Contended for their fatherland;
Peasants, whose new-found strength had broke
From manly necks the ignoble yoke,
And beat their fetters into swords,
On equal terms to fight their lords;
And what insurgent rage had gained,
In many a mortal fray maintained;
Marshalled, once more, at Freedom's call,
They came to conquer or to fall,
Where he who conquered, he who fell,
Was deemed a dead or living Tell,
Such virtue had that patriot breathed,
So to the soil his soul bequeathed,
That wheresoe'er his arrows flew,
Heroes in his own likeness grew,
And warriors sprang from every sod,
Which his awakening footstep trod.

And now the work of life and death
Hung on the passing of a breath;
The fire of conflict burned within,
The battle trembled to begin;
Yet, while the Austrians held their ground.
Point for attack was nowhere found;
Where'er the impatient Switzers gazed,
The unbroken line of lances blazed;

That line 'twere suicide to meet,
And perish at their tyrant's feet;
How could they rest within their graves,
And leave their homes, the homes of slaves?
Would not they feel their children tread,
With clanging chains, above their head?

It must not be; this day, this hour,
Annihilates the invader's power;
All Switzerland is in the field;
She will not fly,—she cannot yield,—
She must not fall; her better fate
Here gives her an immortal date.
Few were the numbers she could boast,
But every freeman was a host,
And felt as 'twere a secret known
That one should turn the scale alone,
While each unto himself was he
On whose sole arm hung victory.

It did depend on one indeed;
Behold him,—Arnold Winkelried;
There sounds not to the trump of fame
The echo of a nobler name.
Unmarked he stood amid the throng,
In rumination deep and long,
Till you might see, with sudden grace,
The very thought come o'er his face;
And, by the motion of his form,
Anticipate the bursting storm,
And, by the uplifting of his brow,
Tell where the bolt would strike, and how.

But 'twas no sooner thought than done!
The field was in a moment won;
"Make way for liberty!" he cried,
Then ran, with arms extended wide,
As if his dearest friend to clasp;
Ten spears he swept within his grasp;
"Make way for liberty!" he cried.
Their keen points crossed from side to side;
He bowed amidst them like a tree,
And thus made way for liberty.

Swift to the breach his comrades fly,
"Make way for liberty!" they cry,
And through the Austrian phalanx dart,
As rushed the spears through Arnold's heart,
While instantaneous as his fall,
Rout, ruin, panic, seized them all;
An earthquake could not overthrow
A city with a surer blow.

Thus Switzerland again was free;
Thus Death made way for Liberty!

JAMES MONTGOMERY.

Life, I Know Not What Thou Art.

LIFE! I know not what thou art,
But know that thou and I must part;
And when, or how, or where we met
I own to me's a secret yet.
Life! we've been long together
Through pleasant and through cloudy weather;

'Tis hard to part when friends are dear—
Perhaps 'twill cost a sigh, a tear;
—Then steal away, give little warning,
Choose thine own time;
Say not Good Night,—but in some brighter clime
Bid me Good Morning.

A. L. BARBAULD.

Mercy.

"Mercy," an excerpt from "The Merchant of Venice," "Polonius'
Advice," from "Hamlet," and Antony's Speech," from "Julius Cæsar"
(all fragments from Shakespeare, 1564–1616), find a place in this book
because a well-known New York teacher—one who is unremitting in his
efforts to raise the good taste and character of his pupils—says: "A
book of poetry could not be complete without these extracts."

THE quality of mercy is not strain'd;
It droppeth as the gentle rain from Heaven
Upon the place beneath: it is twice bless'd;
It blesseth him that gives, and him that takes:
'Tis mightiest in the mightiest; it becomes
The throned monarch better than his crown:
His scepter shows the force of temporal power,
The attribute to awe and majesty,
Wherein doth sit the dread and fear of kings;
But mercy is above his sceptered sway;
It is enthroned in the hearts of kings,
It is an attribute to God himself;
And earthly power doth then show likest God's
When mercy seasons justice.

SHAKESPEARE ("Merchant of Venice").

Polonius' Advice.

SEE thou character. Give thy thoughts no tongue,
Nor any unproportion'd thought his act.
Be thou familiar, but by no means vulgar:
The friends thou hast, and their adoption tried,
Grapple them to thy soul with hoops of steel;
But do not dull thy palm with entertainment
Of each new-hatch'd, unfledg'd comrade. Beware
Of entrance to a quarrel; but, being in,
Bear 't that th' opposed may beware of thee.
Give every man thine ear, but few thy voice:
Take each man's censure, but reserve thy judg-
    ment.
Costly thy habit as thy purse can buy,
But not express'd in fancy; rich, not gaudy:
For the apparel oft proclaims the man.
Neither a borrower nor a lender be;
For loan oft loses both itself and friend,
And borrowing dulls the edge of husbandry.
This above all: to thine own self be true;
And it must follow, as the night the day,
Thou canst not then be false to any man.

SHAKESPEARE ("Hamlet").

A Fragment from Mark Antony's Speech.

THIS was the noblest Roman of them all:
All the conspirators, save only he,
Did that they did in envy of great Cæsar;
He only, in a general honest thought

And common good to all, made one of them.
His life was gentle; and the elements
So mix'd in him, that Nature might stand up,
And say to all the world, "This was a man!"

SHAKESPEARE ("Julius Cæsar").

The Skylark.

BIRD of the wilderness,
Blithesome and cumberless,
Sweet be thy matin o'er moorland and lea!
Emblem of happiness,
Blest is thy dwelling-place—
Oh, to abide in the desert with thee!

Wild is thy lay and loud,
Far in the downy cloud,
Love gives it energy, love gave it birth.
Where, on thy dewy wing,
Where art thou journeying?
Thy lay is in heaven, thy love is on earth.

O'er fell and fountain sheen,
O'er moor and mountain green,
O'er the red streamer that heralds the day,
Over the cloudlet dim,
Over the rainbow's rim,
Musical cherub, soar, singing, away!

Then, when the gloaming comes,
Low in the heather blooms
Sweet will thy welcome and bed of love be!

Emblem of happiness,
  Blest is thy dwelling-place—
Oh, to abide in the desert with thee!
THOMAS HOGG.

The Choir Invisible.

"The Choir Invisible" (by George Eliot, 1819-80) is a fitting exposition in poetry of this "Shakespeare of prose."

O, MAY I join the choir invisible
Of those immortal dead who live again
In minds made better by their presence; live
In pulses stirred to generosity,
In deeds of daring rectitude, in scorn
Of miserable aims that end with self,
In thoughts sublime that pierce the night like stars,
And with their mild persistence urge men's minds
To vaster issues.
            May I reach
That purest heaven,—be to other souls
The cup of strength in some great agony,
Enkindle generous ardour, feed pure love,
Beget the smiles that have no cruelty,
Be the sweet presence of good diffused,
And in diffusion ever more intense!
So shall I join the choir invisible,
Whose music is the gladness of the world.
GEORGE ELIOT.

The World Is Too Much With Us.

"The World Is Too Much With Us," by Wordsworth (1770–1850), is perhaps the greatest sonnet ever written. It is true that "the eyes of the soul" are blinded by a surfeit of worldly "goods." "I went to the Lake District" (England), said John Burroughs, "to see what kind of a country could produce a Wordsworth." Of course he found simple houses, simple people, barren moors, heather-clad mountains, wild flowers, calm lakes, plain, rugged simplicity.

THE world is too much with us; late and soon,
  Getting and spending, we lay waste our powers;
  Little we see in Nature that is ours.
We have given our hearts away, a sordid boon!
This sea, that bares her bosom to the moon,
  The winds that will be howling at all hours,
  And are up-gathered now like sleeping flowers—
For this, for everything, we are out of tune;
It moves us not.   Great God! I'd rather be
A pagan, suckled in a creed outworn,
So might I, standing on this pleasant lea,
  Have glimpses that would make me less forlorn;
Have sight of Proteus, rising from the sea,
  Or hear old Triton blow his wreathèd horn.

WILLIAM WORDSWORTH.

On His Blindness.

"Sonnet on His Blindness" (by John Milton, 1608–74). This is the most stately and pathetic sonnet in existence. The soul enduring enforced idleness and loss of power without repining. Inactivity made to serve a higher end.

"All service ranks the same with God!
There is no first or last."

WHEN I consider how my light is spent
  Ere half my days, in this dark world and wide,
  And that one talent which is death to hide,

Lodg'd with me useless, though my soul more bent
To serve therewith my Maker, and present
  My true account, lest He, returning, chide;
  Doth God exact day-labour, light denied?
I fondly ask: but Patience, to prevent
That murmur, soon replies, God doth not need
  Either man's work, or His own gifts; who best
  Bear His mild yoke, they serve Him best; His
    state
Is kingly; thousands at His bidding speed,
  And post o'er land and ocean without rest;
  They also serve who only stand and wait.

JOHN MILTON.

She Was a Phantom of Delight.

"She Was a Phantom of Delight" (by William Wordsworth, 1770–1850) is included here because it is a picture of woman as she should be, not made dainty by finery, but by fine ideals—

> "And not too good
> For human nature's daily food.

SHE was a Phantom of delight
When first she gleamed upon my sight;
A lovely Apparition, sent
To be a moment's ornament;
Her eyes as stars of Twilight fair;
Like Twilight's, too, her dusky hair:
But all things else about her drawn
From May-time and the cheerful Dawn.
A dancing Shape, an Image gay,
To haunt, to startle, and waylay.

I saw her upon nearer view,
A Spirit, yet a Woman too!

Her household motions light and free,
And steps of virgin liberty;
A countenance in which did meet
Sweet records, promises as sweet;
A Creature not too bright or good
For human nature's daily food;
For transient sorrows, simple wiles,
Praise, blame, love, kisses, tears, and smiles.

And now I see with eye serene
The very pulse of the machine;
A Being breathing thoughtful breath,
A Traveller between life and death:
The reason firm, the temperate will,
Endurance, foresight, strength, and skill;
A perfect Woman, nobly planned,
To warn, to comfort, and command;
And yet a Spirit still, and bright,
With something of angelic light.

WILLIAM WORDSWORTH.

Elegy Written in a Country Churchyard.

"Elegy Written in a Country Churchyard" (Gray, 1716-71). I once drove from Windsor Castle through Eton, down the long hedge-bound road which passes the estate of William Penn's descendants to Stoke Pogis, the little churchyard where this poem was written. They were trimming a great yew-tree under which Gray was said to have written this poem. The scene is one of peace and quiet. The "elegy" was a favourite form of poem with the ancients, but Gray is said to have reached the climax among poets in this style of verse. The great line of the poem is:

"The path of glory leads but to the grave."
It would almost seem that poetry has for its greatest mission the lesson of a proper humility.

THE curfew tolls the knell of parting day,
The lowing herd winds slowly o'er the lea,

The plowman homeward plods his weary way,
  And leaves the world to darkness and to me.

Now fades the glimmering landscape on the sight,
  And all the air a solemn stillness holds,
Save where the beetle wheels his droning flight,
  And drowsy tinklings lull the distant folds.

Save that from yonder ivy-mantled tow'r
  The moping owl does to the moon complain
Of such as, wand'ring near her secret bow'r,
  Molest her ancient solitary reign.

Beneath those rugged elms, that yew-tree's shade,
  Where heaves the turf in many a mould'ring
    heap,
Each in his narrow cell forever laid,
  The rude Forefathers of the hamlet sleep.

The breezy call of incense-breathing morn,
  The swallow twitt'ring from the straw-built shed,
The cock's shrill clarion, or the echoing horn,
  No more shall rouse them from their lowly bed.

For them no more the blazing hearth shall burn,
  Or busy housewife ply her evening care:
No children run to lisp their sire's return,
  Or climb his knees the envied kiss to share.

Oft did the harvest to their sickle yield,
  Their furrow oft the stubborn glebe has broke;
How jocund did they drive their team afield!
  How bow'd the woods beneath their sturdy
    stroke!

Let not Ambition mock their useful toil,
  Their homely joys, and destiny obscure;
Nor Grandeur hear with a disdainful smile,
  The short and simple annals of the Poor.

The boast of heraldry, the pomp of pow'r,
  And all that beauty, all that wealth e'er gave,
Await alike th' inevitable hour.
  The paths of glory lead but to the grave.

Forgive, ye Proud, th' involuntary fault
  If Memory to these no trophies raise,
Where thro' the long-drawn aisle and fretted vault
  The pealing anthem swells the note of praise.

Can storied urn or animated bust
  Back to its mansion call the fleeting breath?
Can Honour's voice provoke the silent dust,
  Or Flatt'ry soothe the dull cold ear of Death?

Perhaps in this neglected spot is laid
  Some heart once pregnant with celestial fire,
Hands that the rod of empire might have sway'd
  Or waked to ecstasy the living lyre.

But Knowledge to their eyes her ample page
  Rich with the spoils of time did ne'er unroll;
Chill Penury repress'd their noble rage,
  And froze the genial current of the soul.

Full many a gem of purest ray serene,
  The dark unfathom'd caves of ocean bear:
Full many a flower is born to blush unseen,
  And waste its sweetness on the desert air.

Some village-Hampden, that with dauntless breast
    The little tyrant of his fields withstood;
Some mute inglorious Milton here may rest,
    Some Cromwell guiltless of his country's blood.

Th' applause of list'ning senates to command,
    The threats of pain and ruin to despise,
To scatter plenty o'er a smiling land,
    And read their history in a nation's eyes,

Their lot forbad: nor circumscribed alone
    Their growing virtues, but their crimes confined
Forbad to wade through slaughter to a throne,
    And shut the gates of mercy on mankind,

The struggling pangs of conscious truth to hide,
    To quench the blushes of ingenuous shame,
Or heap the shrine of Luxury and Pride
    With incense, kindled at the Muse's flame.

Far from the madding crowd's ignoble strife,
    Their sober wishes never learn'd to stray;
Along the cool sequester'd vale of life
    They kept the noiseless tenour of their way.

Yet e'en those bones from insult to protect
    Some frail memorial still erected nigh,
With uncouth rhimes and shapeless sculpture
    deck'd,
    Implores the passing tribute of a sigh.

Their name, their years, spelt by th' unletter'd
    Muse,
    The place of fame and elegy supply:

And many a holy text around she strews
    That teach the rustic moralist to die.

For who to dumb forgetfulness a prey,
    This pleasing anxious being e'er resign'd,
Left the warm precincts of the cheerful day,
    Nor cast one longing, ling'ring look behind?

On some fond breast the parting soul relies,
    Some pious drops the closing eye requires;
E'en from the tomb the voice of Nature cries,
    E'en in our ashes live their wonted fires.

For thee, who, mindful of th' unhonour'd dead,
    Dost in these lines their artless tale relate;
If chance, by lonely Contemplation led,
    Some kindred spirit shall inquire thy fate,

Haply some hoary-headed swain may say,
    "Oft have we seen him at the peep of dawn
Brushing with hasty steps the dews away,
    To meet the sun upon the upland lawn.

"There at the foot of yonder nodding beech
    That wreathes its old fantastic roots so high,
His listless length at noon-tide would he stretch,
    And pore upon the brook that babbles by.

"Hard by yon wood, now smiling as in scorn,
    Muttering his wayward fancies he would rove;
Now drooping, woeful wan, like one forlorn,
    Or crazed with care, or cross'd in hopeless love.

"One morn I miss'd him on the custom'd hill,
    Along the heath, and near his favourite tree;
Another came; nor yet beside the rill,
    Nor up the lawn, nor at the wood was he.

"The next with dirges due in sad array
    Slow thro' the church-way path we saw him
        borne.
Approach and read (for thou canst read) the lay,
    Graved on the stone beneath yon agèd thorn."

THE EPITAPH.

Here rests his head upon the lap of Earth
    A Youth to Fortune and to Fame unknown:
Fair Science frown'd not on his humble birth,
    And Melancholy mark'd him for her own.

Large was his bounty, and his soul sincere,
    Heaven did a recompense as largely send:
He gave to Mis'ry all he had, a tear:
    He gain'd from Heav'n ('twas all he wish'd) a
        friend.

No farther seek his merits to disclose,
    Or draw his frailties from their dread abode,
(There they alike in trembling hope repose,)
    The bosom of his Father and his God.

THOMAS GRAY.

Rabbi Ben Ezra.

"Rabbi Ben Ezra" (by Robert Browning, 1812–89). Youth is for dispute and age for counsel; each year, each period of a man's life is but the necessary step to the next. Youth is an uncertain thing to bank on.

"Grow old along with me!
The best is yet to be,
The last of life for which the first was made."

"Rabbi Ben Ezra" is a plea for each period in life. Aspiration is the keynote.

" . . . Trust God; see all, nor be afraid!"

GROW old along with me!
The best is yet to be,
The last of life, for which the first was made:
Our times are in His hand
Who saith, "A whole I plann'd,
Youth shows but half; trust God: see all nor be
afraid!"

Not that, amassing flowers,
Youth sigh'd, "Which rose make ours,
Which lily leave and then as best recall?"
Not that, admiring stars,
It yearn'd, "Nor Jove, nor Mars;
Mine be some figured flame which blends, tran-
scends them all!"

Not for such hopes and fears
Annulling youth's brief years,
Do I remonstrate: folly wide the mark!
Rather I prize the doubt
Low kinds exist without,
Finish'd and finite clods. untroubled by a spark.

Poor vaunt of life indeed,
Were man but formed to feed
On joy, to solely seek and find and feast:
Such feasting ended, then
As sure an end to men;
Irks care the crop-full bird? Frets doubt the
maw-cramm'd beast?

Rejoice we are allied
To That which doth provide
And not partake, effect and not receive!
A spark disturbs our clod;
Nearer we hold of God
Who gives, than of His tribes that take, I must
believe.

Then, welcome each rebuff
That turns earth's smoothness rough,
Each sting, that bids nor sit nor stand, but go!
Be our joys three parts pain!
Strive, and hold cheap the strain;
Learn, nor account the pang; dare, never grudge
the throe!

For thence,—a paradox
Which comforts while it mocks,—
Shall life succeed in that it seems to fail:
What I aspired to be,
And was not, comforts me:
A brute I might have been, but would not sink i'
the scale.

What is he but a brute
Whose flesh has soul to suit,
Whose spirit works lest arms and legs want play?

To man, propose this test—
Thy body at its best,
How far can that project thy soul on its lone way?

Yet gifts should prove their use:
I own the Past profuse
Of power each side, perfection every turn:
Eyes, ears took in their dole,
Brain treasured up the whole:
Should not the heart beat once "How good to
live and learn?"

Not once beat "Praise be Thine!
I see the whole design,
I, who saw power, see now love perfect too:
Perfect I call Thy plan:
Thanks that I was a man!
Maker, remake, complete,—I trust what Thou
shalt do!"

For pleasant is this flesh;
Our soul, in its rose-mesh
Pull'd ever to the earth, still yearns for rest;
Would we some prize might hold
To match those manifold
Possessions of the brute,—gain most, as we did
best!

Let us not always say,
"Spite of this flesh to-day
I strove, made head, gain'd ground upon the
whole!"

As the bird wings and sings,
Let us cry, "All good things
Are ours, nor soul helps flesh more, now, than
flesh helps soul!"

Therefore I summon age
To grant youth's heritage,
Life's struggle having so far reach'd its term:
Thence shall I pass, approved
A man, for aye removed
From the develop'd brute; a god though in the
germ.

And I shall thereupon
Take rest, ere I be gone
Once more on my adventure brave and new:
Fearless and unperplex'd,
When I wage battle next,
What weapons to select, what armour to indue.

Youth ended, I shall try
My gain or loss thereby;
Leave the fire ashes, what survives is gold:
And I shall weigh the same,
Give life its praise or blame:
Young, all lay in dispute; I shall know, being old.

For note, when evening shuts,
A certain moment cuts
The deed off, calls the glory from the gray:
A whisper from the west
Shoots—"Add this to the rest,
Take it and try its worth: here dies another day."

So, still within this life,
Though lifted o'er its strife,
Let me discern, compare, pronounce at last,
"This rage was right i' the main,
That acquiescence vain:
The Future I may face now I have proved the
Past."

For more is not reserved
To man, with soul just nerved
To act to-morrow what he learns to-day:
Here, work enough to watch
The Master work, and catch
Hints of the proper craft, tricks of the tool's true
play.

As it was better, youth
Should strive, through acts uncouth,
Toward making, than repose on aught found
made:
So, better, age, exempt
From strife, should know, than tempt
Further. Thou waitedest age: wait death nor be
afraid!

Enough now, if the Right
And Good and Infinite
Be named here, as thou callest thy hand thine own,
With knowledge absolute,
Subject to no dispute
From fools that crowded youth, nor let thee feel
alone.

Be there, for once and all,
Sever'd great minds from small,
Announced to each his station in the Past!
Was I, the world arraign'd,
Were they, my soul disdain'd,
Right? Let age speak the truth and give us
peace at last!

Now, who shall arbitrate?
Ten men love what I hate,
Shun what I follow, slight what I receive;
Ten, who in ears and eyes
Match me: we all surmise,
They this thing, and I that: whom shall my soul
believe?

Not on the vulgar mass
Call'd "work," must sentence pass,
Things done, that took the eye and had the price;
O'er which, from level stand,
The low world laid its hand,
Found straightway to its mind, could value in a
trice:

But all, the world's coarse thumb
And finger fail'd to plumb,
So pass'd in making up the main account;
All instincts immature,
All purposes unsure,
That weigh'd not as his work, yet swell'd the
man's amount:

Thoughts hardly to be pack'd
Into a narrow act,
Fancies that broke through language and escaped;

All I could never be,
All, men ignored in me,
This, I was worth to God, whose wheel the pitcher
shaped.

Ay, note that Potter's wheel,
That metaphor! and feel
Why time spins fast, why passive lies our clay,—
Thou, to whom fools propound,
When the wine makes its round,
"Since life fleets, all is change; the Past gone,
seize to-day!"

Fool! All that is, at all,
Lasts ever, past recall;
Earth changes, but thy soul and God stand sure:
What enter'd into thee,
That was, is, and shall be:
Time's wheel runs back or stops: Potter and
clay endure.

He fix'd thee 'mid this dance
Of plastic circumstance,
This Present, thou, forsooth, wouldst fain arrest:
Machinery just meant
To give thy soul its bent,
Try thee and turn thee forth, sufficiently im-
press'd.

What though the earlier grooves
Which ran the laughing loves
Around thy base, no longer pause and press?

What though, about thy rim,
Scull-things in order grim
Grow out, in graver mood, obey the sterner stress?

Look not thou down but up!
To uses of a cup,
The festal board, lamp's flash and trumpet's peal,
The new wine's foaming flow,
The master's lips aglow!
Thou, heaven's consummate cup, what need'st
thou with earth's wheel?

But I need, now as then,
Thee, God, who mouldest men;
And since, not even while the whirl was worst
Did I,—to the wheel of life
With shapes and colours rife,
Bound dizzily,—mistake my end, to slake Thy
thirst:

So, take and use Thy work:
Amend what flaws may lurk,
What strain o' the stuff, what warpings past the
aim!
My times be in Thy hand!
Perfect the cup as plann'd!
Let age approve of youth, and death complete
the same!

ROBERT BROWNING.

Prospice.

"Prospice," by Robert Browning (1812-89), is the greatest death-song ever written. It is a battle-song and a pæan of victory.

> "The journey is done, the summit attained,
> And the strong man must go."
> "I would hate that Death bandaged my eyes and forbore,
> And bade me creep past."
> "No! let me taste the whole of it."
> "The reward of all."

This poem is included in this book because these lines are enough to reconcile any one to any fate.

FEAR death?—to feel the fog in my throat,
　　The mist in my face,
When the snows begin, and the blasts denote
　　I am nearing the place,
The power of the night, the press of the storm,
　　The post of the foe;
Where he stands, the Arch Fear in a visible form,
　　Yet the strong man must go:
For the journey is done and the summit attained,
　　And the barriers fall,
Though a battle's to fight ere a guerdon be gained,
　　The reward of it all.
I was ever a fighter, so—one fight more.
　　The best and the last!
I would hate that death bandaged my eyes, and
　　forebore,
　　And bade me creep past.
No! let me taste the whole of it, fare like my peers
　　The heroes of old,
Bear the brunt, in a minute pay glad life's arrears
　　Of pain, darkness, and cold.
For sudden the worst turns the best to the brave,
　　The black minute's at end,

And the elements' rage, the fiend-voices that rave
    Shall dwindle, shall blend,
Shall change, shall become first a peace out of
    pain,
    Then a light, then thy breast,
O thou soul of my soul! I shall clasp thee again,
    And with God be the rest!

ROBERT BROWNING.

Recessional.

"The Recessional" (by Rudyard Kipling, 1865–) is one of the most popular poems of this century. It is a warning to an age and a nation drunk with power, a rebuke to materialistic tendencies and boastfulness, a protest against pride.

"Reverence is the master-key of knowledge."

GOD of our fathers, known of old—
    Lord of our far-flung battle-line—
Beneath whose awful Hand we hold
    Dominion over palm and pine—
Lord God of Hosts, be with us yet,
Lest we forget—lest we forget!

The tumult and the shouting dies—
    The captains and the kings depart—
Still stands Thine ancient Sacrifice,
    An humble and a contrite heart.
Lord God of Hosts, be with us yet,
Lest we forget—lest we forget!

Far-called our navies melt away—
    On dune and headland sinks the fire—
Lo, all our pomp of yesterday
    Is one with Nineveh and Tyre!

Judge of the Nations, spare us yet,
Lest we forget—lest we forget!

If, drunk with sight of power, we loose
    Wild tongues that have not Thee in awe—
Such boasting as the Gentiles use
    Or lesser breeds without the Law—
Lord God of Hosts, be with us yet,
Lest we forget—lest we forget!

For heathen heart that puts her trust
    In reeking tube and iron shard—
All valiant dust that builds on dust,
    And guarding calls not Thee to guard—
For frantic boast and foolish word,
Thy mercy on Thy People, Lord! Amen.
                  RUDYARD KIPLING.

Ozymandias of Egypt.

"Ozymandias of Egypt," by Percy Bysshe Shelley (1792–1822). This sonnet is a rebuke to the insolent pride of kings and empires. It is extremely picturesque. It finds a place here because more elderly scholars of good judgment are pleased with it. I remember an old gray-haired scholar in Chicago who often recited it to his friends merely because it touched his fancy.

I MET a traveller from an antique land
Who said: "Two vast and trunkless legs of stone
Stand in the desert. Near them on the sand,
Half sunk, a shatter'd visage lies, whose frown
And wrinkled lip and sneer of cold command
Tell that its sculptor well those passions read
Which yet survive, stamp'd on these lifeless
    things,
The hand that mock'd them and the heart that fed;

And on the pedestal these words appear:
'My name is Ozymandias, king of kings:
Look on my works, ye Mighty, and despair!'
Nothing beside remains.   Round the decay
Of that colossal wreck, boundless and bare,
The lone and level sands stretch far away."

PERCY BYSSHE SHELLEY.

Mortality.

"Mortality" (by William Knox, 1789-1825) is always quoted as Lincoln's favourite poem.

O WHY should the spirit of mortal be proud?
Like a fast-flitting meteor, a fast-flying cloud,
A flash of the lightning, a break of the wave,
He passes from life to his rest in the grave.

The leaves of the oak and the willow shall fade,
Be scattered around and together be laid;
And the young and the old, and the low and the
    high,
Shall moulder to dust and together shall lie.

The child that a mother attended and loved,
The mother that infant's affection that proved,
The husband that mother and infant that blessed,
Each, all, are away to their dwelling of rest.

The maid on whose cheek, on whose brow, in
    whose eye,
Shone beauty and pleasure,—her triumphs are by;
And the memory of those that beloved her and
    praised
Are alike from the minds of the living erased

The hand of the king that the scepter hath borne,
The brow of the priest that the miter hath worn,
The eye of the sage, and the heart of the brave,
Are hidden and lost in the depths of the grave.

The peasant whose lot was to sow and to reap,
The herdsman who climbed with his goats to the
    steep,
The beggar that wandered in search of his bread,
Have faded away like the grass that we tread.

The saint that enjoyed the communion of heaven,
The sinner that dared to remain unforgiven,
The wise and the foolish, the guilty and just,
Have quietly mingled their bones in the dust.

So the multitude goes, like the flower and the weed
That wither away to let others succeed;
So the multitude comes, even those we behold,
To repeat every tale that hath often been told.

For we are the same that our fathers have been;
We see the same sights that our fathers have seen,—
We drink the same stream, and we feel the same sun,
And we run the same course that our fathers have
    run.

The thoughts we are thinking, our fathers would
    think;
From the death we are shrinking from, they too
    would shrink;
To the life we are clinging to, they too would cling;
But it speeds from the earth like a bird on the wing.

They loved, but their story we cannot unfold;
They scorned, but the heart of the haughty is cold;
They grieved, but no wail from their slumbers
    may come;
They enjoyed, but the voice of their gladness is
    dumb.

They died, ay! they died! and we things that are
    now,
Who walk on the turf that lies over their brow,
Who make in their dwellings a transient abode,
Meet the changes they met on their pilgrimage
    road.

Yea! hope and despondence, and pleasure and
    pain,
Are mingled together like sunshine and rain;
And the smile and the tear, and the song and the
    dirge,
Still follow each other, like surge upon surge.

'Tis the wink of an eye, 'tis the draught of a breath,
From the blossom of health to the paleness of
    death,
From the gilded saloon to the bier and the shroud,—
O why should the spirit of mortal be proud?

                    WILLIAM KNOX.

On First Looking Into Chapman's "Homer."

"On First Looking Into Chapman's 'Homer,'" by John Keats (1795-1821). The last four lines of this sonnet form the most tremendous climax in literature. The picture is as vivid as if done with a brush. Every great book, every great poem is a new world, an undiscovered country. Every learned person is a whole territory, a universe of new thought. Every one who does anything with a heart for it, every specialist every one, however simple, who is strenuous and genuine, is a "new discovery." Let us give credit to the smallest planet that is true to its own orbit.

MUCH have I travell'd in the realms of gold,
And many goodly states and kingdoms seen;
Round many western islands have I been
Which bards in fealty to Apollo hold.

Oft of one wide expanse had I been told
That deep-brow'd Homer ruled as his demesne:
Yet did I never breathe its pure serene
Till I heard Chapman speak out loud and bold:

Then felt I like some watcher of the skies
When a new planet swims into his ken;
Or like stout Cortez when with eagle eyes

He stared at the Pacific—and all his men
Look'd at each other with a wild surmise—
Silent, upon a peak in Darien.

JOHN KEATS.

Hervé Riel.

"Hervé Riel" (by Robert Browning, 1812-89) is a poem for older boys. Here is a hero who does a great deed simply as a part of his day's work. He puts no value on what he has done, because he could have done no other way.

ON the sea and at the Hogue, sixteen hundred
      ninety-two,
Did the English fight the French—woe to France!

And, the thirty-first of May, helter-skelter through
    the blue,
Like a crowd of frightened porpoises a shoal of
    sharks pursue,
  Came crowding ship on ship to St. Malo on the
    Rance,
       With the English fleet in view.

'Twas the squadron that escaped, with the victor
    in full chase,
  First and foremost of the drove, in his great
    ship, Damfreville ;
      Close on him fled, great and small,
      Twenty-two good ships in all;
      And they signalled to the place,
      "Help the winners of a race!
  Get us guidance, give us harbour, take us quick—
    or, quicker still,
      Here's the English can and will!"

Then the pilots of the place put out brisk and
    leaped on board:
  "Why, what hope or chance have ships like
    these to pass?" laughed they;
  "Rocks to starboard, rocks to port, all the
    passage scarred and scored,
Shall the *Formidable* here, with her twelve and
    eighty guns,
Think to make the river-mouth by the single
    narrow way,
Trust to enter where 'tis ticklish for a craft of
    twenty tons,

And with flow at full beside?
Now 'tis slackest ebb of tide.
Reach the mooring! Rather say,
While rock stands or water runs,
Not a ship will leave the bay!"

Then was called a council straight;
Brief and bitter the debate:
"Here's the English at our heels; would you have
them take in tow
All that's left us of the fleet, linked together stern
and bow,
For a prize to Plymouth Sound?—
Better run the ships aground!"
(Ended Damfreville his speech.)
"Not a minute more to wait!
Let the captains all and each
Shove ashore, then blow up, burn the vessels on
the beach!
France must undergo her fate.

"Give the word!"—But no such word
Was ever spoke or heard;
For up stood, for out stepped, for in struck amid
all these—
A captain? A lieutenant? A mate—first, second,
third?
No such man of mark, and meet
With his betters to compete!
But a simple Breton sailor pressed by Tourville
for the fleet—
A poor coasting pilot he, Hervé Riel, the Croisic-
kese.

And "What mockery or malice have we here?"
    cries Hervé Riel:
 "Are you mad, you Malouins?   Are you cow-
    ards, fools, or rogues?
Talk to me of rocks and shoals, me who took the
    soundings, tell
On my fingers every bank, every shallow, every
    swell,
   'Twixt the offing here and Grève where the river
    disembogues?
Are you bought by English gold?   Is it love the
    lying's for?
       Morn and eve, night and day,
       Have I piloted your bay,
Entered free and anchored fast at the foot of
    Solidor.
 Burn the fleet and ruin France?   That were
    worse than fifty Hogues!
Sirs, they know I speak the truth!   Sirs, believe
    me there's a way!
       Only let me lead the line,
        Have the biggest ship to steer,
        Get this *Formidable* clear,
       Make the others follow mine,
And I lead them, most and least, by a passage I
    know well,
       Right to Solidor past Grève,
        And there lay them safe and sound;
       And if one ship misbehave,
        —Keel so much as grate the ground,
Why, I've nothing but my life,—here's my head!"
    cries Hervé Riel.

Not a minute more to wait
"Steer us in, then, small and great!
Take the helm, lead the line, save the squadron!"
      cried its chief.
            Captains, give the sailor place!
                  He is Admiral, in brief.
            Still the north wind, by God's grace!
            See the noble fellow's face
            As the big ship, with a bound,
            Clears the entry like a hound,
Keeps the passage as its inch of way were the wide
      sea's profound!
                  See, safe through shoal and rock,
                  How they follow in a flock,
Not a ship that misbehaves, not a keel that grates
      the ground,
                  Not a spar that comes to grief!
                  The peril, see, is past,
                  All are harboured to the last,
And just as Hervé Riel hollas "Anchor!"—sure
      as fate,
                  Up the English come—too late!

                  So, the storm subsides to calm:
                        They see the green trees wave
                        On the heights o'erlooking Grève.
                  Hearts that bled are stanched with balm.
                  "Just our rapture to enhance,
                        Let the English rake the bay,
                  Gnash their teeth and glare askance
                        As they cannonade away!
'Neath rampired Solidor pleasant riding on the
      Rance!"

How hope succeeds despair on each Captain's
        countenance!
        Out burst all with one accord,
         "This is Paradise for Hell!
         Let France, let France's King
         Thank the man that did the thing!"
        What a shout, and all one word,
         "Hervé Riel!"
        As he stepped in front once more,
         Not a symptom of surprise
         In the frank blue Breton eyes,
        Just the same man as before.

        Then said Damfreville, "My friend,
        I must speak out at the end,
         Though I find the speaking hard.
        Praise is deeper than the lips:
        You have saved the King his ships,
         You must name your own reward.
        'Faith, our sun was near eclipse!
        Demand whate'er you will,
        France remains your debtor still.
Ask to heart's content and have! or my name's not
        Damfreville."

        Then a beam of fun outbroke
        On the bearded mouth that spoke,
        As the honest heart laughed through
        Those frank eyes of Breton blue:
        "Since I needs must say my say,
        Since on board the duty's done,
And from Malo Roads to Croisic Point, what is it
        but a run?—

Since 'tis ask and have, I may—
　　Since the others go ashore—
　Come!　A good whole holiday!
Leave to go and see my wife, whom I call the
　　Belle Aurore!"
That he asked and that he got,—nothing more.

　　Name and deed alike are lost:
　　Not a pillar nor a post
In his Croisic keeps alive the feat as it befell;
　　Not a head in white and black
　　On a single fishing smack,
In memory of the man but for whom had gone to
　　wrack
　All that France saved from the fight whence
　　England bore the bell.
　　Go to Paris: rank on rank
　　　Search the heroes flung pell-mell
　　On the Louvre, face and flank!
You shall look long enough ere you come to
　　Hervé Riel,
　　So, for better and for worse,
　　Hervé Riel, accept my verse!
In my verse, Hervé Riel, do thou once more
Save the squadron, honour France, love thy wife
　　the Belle Aurore!

ROBERT BROWNING.

The Problem.

"The Problem" (by Ralph Waldo Emerson, 1803–80) is quoted from one end of the world to the other. Emerson teaches one lesson above all others, that each soul must work out for itself its latent force, its own individual expression, and that with a "sad sincerity." "The bishop of the soul" can do no more.

I LIKE a church; I like a cowl;
I love a prophet of the soul;
And on my heart monastic aisles
Fall like sweet strains, or pensive smiles:
Yet not for all his faith can see
Would I that cowlèd churchman be.
Why should the vest on him allure,
Which I could not on me endure?

Not from a vain or shallow thought
His awful Jove young Phidias brought;
Never from lips of cunning fell
The thrilling Delphic oracle;
Out from the heart of nature rolled
The burdens of the Bible old;
The litanies of nations came,
Like the volcano's tongue of flame,
Up from the burning core below,—
The canticles of love and woe:
The hand that rounded Peter's dome
And groined the aisles of Christian Rome
Wrought in a sad sincerity;
Himself from God he could not free;
He builded better than he knew;
The conscious stone to beauty grew.

Knowst thou what wove yon woodbird's nest
Of leaves and feathers from her breast?

Or how the fish outbuilt her shell,
Painting with morn each annual cell?
Or how the sacred pine-tree adds
To her old leaves new myriads?
Such and so grew these holy piles,
While love and terror laid the tiles.
Earth proudly wears the Parthenon,
As the best gem upon her zone,
And Morning opes with haste her lids
To gaze upon the Pyramids;
O'er England's abbeys bends the sky,
As on its friends, with kindred eye;
For out of Thought's interior sphere
These wonders rose to upper air;
And Nature gladly gave them place,
Adopted them into her race,
And granted them an equal date
With Andes and with Ararat.

These temples grew as grows the grass;
Art might obey, but not surpass.
The passive Master lent his hand
To the vast soul that o'er him planned;
And the same power that reared the shrine
Bestrode the tribes that knelt within.
Ever the fiery Pentecost
Girds with one flame the countless host,
Trances the heart through chanting choirs,
And through the priest the mind inspires.
The word unto the prophet spoken
Was writ on tables yet unbroken;
The word by seers or sibyls told,
In groves of oak, or fanes of gold,

Still floats upon the morning wind,
Still whispers to the willing mind.
One accent of the Holy Ghost
The heedless world hath never lost.
I know what say the fathers wise,—
The Book itself before me lies,
Old Chrysostom, best Augustine,
And he who blent both in his line,
The younger Golden Lips or mines,
Taylor, the Shakespeare of divines.
His words are music in my ear,
I see his cowlèd portrait dear;
And yet, for all his faith could see,
I would not the good bishop be.

RALPH WALDO EMERSON.

To America.

"To America," included by permission of the Poet Laureate, is a good poem and a great poem. It is a keen thrust at the common practice of teaching American children to hate the English of these days on account of the actions of a silly old king dead a hundred years. Alfred Austin deserves great credit for this poem.

WHAT is the voice I hear
    On the winds of the western sea?
Sentinel, listen from out Cape Clear
    And say what the voice may be.
'Tis a proud free people calling loud to a people
    proud and free.

And it says to them: "Kinsmen, hail!
    We severed have been too long.
Now let us have done with a worn-out tale—
    The tale of an ancient wrong—

And our friendship last long as our love doth and
    be stronger than death is strong."

     Answer them, sons of the self-same race,
       And blood of the self-same clan;
     Let us speak with each other face to face
       And answer as man to man,
And loyally love and trust each other as none but
    free men can.

     Now fling them out to the breeze,
       Shamrock, Thistle, and Rose,
     And the Star-spangled Banner unfurl with
       these—
     A message to friends and foes
Wherever the sails of peace are seen and wherever
    the war-wind blows—

     A message to bond and thrall to wake,
       For wherever we come, we twain,
     The throne of the tyrant shall rock and quake,
       And his menace be void and vain;
For you are lords of a strong land and we are lords
    of the main.

     Yes, this is the voice of the bluff March gale;
       We severed have been too long,
     But now we have done with a worn-out tale—
       The tale of an ancient wrong—
And our friendship last long as love doth last and
    stronger than death is strong.
                   ALFRED AUSTIN.

The English Flag.

It is quite true that the English flag stands for freedom the world over. Wherever it floats almost any one is safe, whether English or not.

[Above the portico the Union Jack remained fluttering in the flames for some time, but ultimately when it fell the crowds rent the air with shouts, and seemed to see significance in the incident.—*Daily Papers*.]

Winds of the World, give answer? They are
   whimpering to and fro—
And what should they know of England who only
   England know?—
The poor little street-bred people that vapour and
   fume and brag,
They are lifting their heads in the stillness to yelp
   at the English Flag!

Must we borrow a clout from the Boer—to plaster
   anew with dirt?
An Irish liar's bandage, or an English coward's
   shirt?
We may not speak of England; her Flag's to sell or
   share.
What is the Flag of England? Winds of the
   World, declare!

The North Wind blew:—"From Bergen my steel-
   shod van-guards go;
I chase your lazy whalers home from the Disko
   floe;

By the great North Lights above me I work the
  will of God,
That the liner splits on the ice-field or the Dogger
  fills with cod.

"I barred my gates with iron, I shuttered my doors
  with flame,
Because to force my ramparts your nutshell navies
  came;
I took the sun from their presence, I cut them
  down with my blast,
And they died, but the Flag of England blew free
  ere the spirit passed.

"The lean white bear hath seen it in the long, long
  Arctic night,
The musk-ox knows the standard that flouts the
  Northern Light:
What is the Flag of England? Ye have but my
  bergs to dare,
Ye have but my drifts to conquer. Go forth, for
  it is there!"

The South Wind sighed:—"From The Virgins my
  mid-sea course was ta'en
Over a thousand islands lost in an idle main,
Where the sea-egg flames on the coral and the
  long-backed breakers croon
Their endless ocean legends to the lazy, locked
  lagoon.

"Strayed amid lonely islets, mazed amid outer keys,
I waked the palms to laughter—I tossed the scud
  in the breeze—

Never was isle so little, never was sea so lone,
But over the scud and the palm-trees an English
    flag was flown.

"I have wrenched it free from the halliard to hang
    for a wisp on the Horn;
I have chased it north to the Lizard—ribboned and
    rolled and torn;
I have spread its fold o'er the dying, adrift in a
    hopeless sea;
I have hurled it swift on the slaver, and seen the
    slave set free.

"My basking sunfish know it, and wheeling alba-
    tross,
Where the lone wave fills with fire beneath the
    Southern Cross.
What is the Flag of England? Ye have but my
    reefs to dare,
Ye have but my seas to furrow. Go forth, for it is
    there!"

The East Wind roared:—"From the Kuriles, the
    Bitter Seas, I come,
And me men call the Home-Wind, for I bring the
    English home.
Look—look well to your shipping! By the breath
    of my mad typhoon
I swept your close-packed Praya and beached your
    best at Kowloon!

"The reeling junks behind me and the racing seas
    before,
I raped your richest roadstead—I plundered Singa-
    pore!

I set my hand on the Hoogli; as a hooded snake
    she rose,
And I flung your stoutest steamers to roost with
    the startled crows.

"Never the lotos closes, never the wild-fowl wake,
But a soul goes out on the East Wind that died for
    England's sake—
Man or woman or suckling, mother or bride or
    maid—
Because on the bones of the English the English
    Flag is stayed.

"The desert-dust hath dimmed it, the flying wild-
    ass knows.
The scared white leopard winds it across the taint-
    less snows.
What is the Flag of England? Ye have but my
    sun to dare,
Ye have but my sands to travel.   Go forth, for it is
    there!"

The West Wind called:—"In squadrons the
    thoughtless galleons fly
That bear the wheat and cattle lest street-bred
    people die.
They make my might their porter, they make my
    house their path,
Till I loose my neck from their rudder and whelm
    them all in my wrath.

"I draw the gliding fog-bank as a snake is drawn
    from the hole;
They bellow one to the other, the frightened ship-
    bells toll,

For day is a drifting terror till I raise the shroud
  with my breath,
And they see strange bows above them and the
  two go locked to death.

"But whether in calm or wrack-wreath, whether
  by dark or day,
I heave them whole to the conger or rip their
  plates away,
First of the scattered legions, under a shrieking
  sky,
Dipping between the rollers, the English Flag
  goes by.

"The dead dumb fog hath wrapped it—the frozen
  dews have kissed—
The naked stars have seen it, a fellow-star in the
  mist.
What is the Flag of England? Ye have but my
  breath to dare,
Ye have but my waves to conquer. Go forth,
  for it is there!"

RUDYARD KIPLING.

The Man With the Hoe.

"The Man With the Hoe" is purely an American product, and every American ought to be proud of it, for we want no such type allowed to be developed in this country as the low-browed peasant of France. This poem is a stroke of genius. The story goes that it so offended a modern plutocrat that he offered a reward of $10,000 to any one who could write an equally good poem in rebuttal. "The Man With the Hoe" has won for Edwin Markham the title of "Poet Laureate of the Labouring Classes."

WRITTEN AFTER SEEING THE PAINTING BY MILLET.

God made man in His own image, in the image of God made He him.
—GENESIS.

BOWED by the weight of centuries he leans
Upon his hoe and gazes on the ground,
The emptiness of ages in his face,
And on his back the burden of the world.
Who made him dead to rapture and despair,
A thing that grieves not and that never hopes,
Stolid and stunned, a brother to the ox?
Who loosened and let down this brutal jaw?
Whose was the hand that slanted back this brow?
Whose breath blew out the light within this brain?

Is this the Thing the Lord God made and gave
To have dominion over sea and land;
To trace the stars and search the heavens for power;
To feel the passion of Eternity?
Is this the Dream He dreamed who shaped the
        suns
And marked their ways upon the ancient deep?
Down all the stretch of Hell to its last gulf
There is no shape more terrible than this—
More tongued with censure of the world's blind
        greed—

More filled with signs and portents for the soul—
More fraught with menace to the universe.

What gulfs between him and the seraphim!
Slave of the wheel of labour, what to him
Are Plato and the swing of Pleiades?
What the long reaches of the peaks of song,
The rift of dawn, the reddening of the rose?
Through this dread shape the suffering ages look;
Time's tragedy is in that aching stoop;
Through this dread shape humanity betrayed,
Plundered, profaned, and disinherited,
Cries protest to the Judges of the World,
A protest that is also prophecy.

O masters, lords, and rulers in all lands,
Is this the handiwork you give to God,
This monstrous thing distorted and soul-quenched?
How will you ever straighten up this shape;
Touch it again with immortality;
Give back the upward looking and the light;
Rebuild in it the music and the dream;
Make right the immemorial infamies,
Perfidious wrongs, immedicable woes?

O masters, lords, and rulers in all lands,
How will the future reckon with this Man?
How answer his brute question in that hour
When whirlwinds of rebellion shake the world?
How will it be with kingdoms and with kings—
With those who shaped him to the thing he is—
When this dumb Terror shall reply to God,
After the silence of the centuries?

EDWIN MARKHAM.

Song of Myself.

"The Song of Myself" is one of Walt Whitman's (1819–92) most characteristic poems. I love the swing and the stride of his great long lines. I love his rough-shod way of trampling down and kicking out of the way the conventionalities that spring up like poisonous mushrooms to make the world a vast labyrinth of petty "proprieties" until everything is nasty. I love the oxygen he pours on the world. I love his genius for brotherliness, his picture of the Negro with rolling eyes and the firelock in the corner. These excerpts are some of his best lines.

I CELEBRATE myself, and sing myself,
And what I assume you shall assume,
For every atom belonging to me as good belongs
    to you.
I loafe and invite my soul,
I lean and loafe at my ease observing a spear of
    summer grass.
My tongue, every atom of my blood, form'd from
    this soil, this air,
Born here of parents born here from parents the
    same, and their parents the same,
I, now thirty-seven years old in perfect health
    begin,
Hoping to cease not till death.

I hail or for good or bad, I permit to speak at
    every hazard,
Nature without check with original energy.

Have you reckon'd a thousand acres much? have
    you reckon'd the earth much?
Have you practised so long to learn to read?
Have you felt so proud to get at the meaning of
    poems?

Stop this day and night with me and you shall
    possess the origin of all poems,
You shall possess the good of the earth and sun
    (there are millions of suns left),
You shall no longer take things at second or third
    hand, nor look through the eyes of the dead,
    nor feed on the specters in books,
You shall not look through my eyes either, nor
    take things from me,
You shall listen to all sides and filter them from
    yourself.

A child said, "*What is the grass?*" fetching it to
    me with full hands;
How could I answer the child? I do not know
    what it is any more than he.
I guess it must be the flag of my disposition, out
    of hopeful green stuff woven.
Or, I guess it is the handkerchief of the Lord,
A scented gift and remembrance designedly dropt,·
Bearing the owner's name some way in the
    corners, that we may see and remark, and say,
    "*Whose?*"

Alone far in the wilds and mountains I hunt,
Wandering amazed at my own lightness and glee,
In the late afternoon choosing a safe spot to pass
    the night,
Kindling a fire and broiling the fresh-kill'd game,
Falling asleep on the gathered leaves with my
    dog and gun by my side.
The Yankee clipper is under her sky-sails, she cuts
    the sparkle and scud,

My eyes settle the land, I bend at her prow or
    shout joyously from the deck.
The boatman and clam-diggers arose early and
    stopt for me,
I tucked my trouser-ends in my boots and went
    and had a good time;
You should have been with us that day round the
    chowder-kettle.

The runaway slave came to my house and stopt
    outside,
I heard his motions crackling the twigs of the
    woodpile,
Through the swung half-door of the kitchen I saw
    him limpsy and weak,
And went where he sat on a log and led him in and
    assured him,
And brought water and fill'd a tub for his sweated
    body and bruis'd feet,
And gave him a room that entered from my own,
    and gave him some coarse clean clothes,
And remember perfectly well his revolving eyes
    and his awkwardness,
And remember putting plasters on the galls of his
    neck and ankles;
He staid with me a week before he was recuperated
    and passed north,
I had him sit next me at table, my firelock lean'd
    in the corner.

I am the poet of the woman the same as the man,
And I say it is as great to be a woman as to be a
    man,

And I say there is nothing greater than the mother
    of men.

I understand the large hearts of heroes,
The courage of present times and all times,
How the skipper saw the crowded and rudderless
    wreck of the steamship, and Death chasing
    it up and down the storm,
How he knuckled tight and gave not back an inch
    and was faithful of days and faithful of nights,
And chalked in large letters on a board, "*Be of
    good cheer, we will not desert you*";
How he follow'd with them and tack'd with them
    three days and would not give it up,
How he saved the drifting company at last,
How the lank loose-gown'd women looked when
    boated from the side of their prepared graves,
How the silent old-faced infants and the lifted
    sick, and the sharp-lipp'd unshaved men;
All this I swallow, it tastes good, I like it well,
    it becomes mine,
I am the man, I suffered, I was there.
The disdain and calmness of martyrs,
The mother of old, condemn'd for a witch, burned
    with dry wood, her children gazing on,
The pounded slave that flags in the race, leans by
    the fence blowing, covered with sweat.
I am the hounded slave, I wince at the bite of the
    dogs,
Hell and despair are upon me, crack and again
    crack the marksmen,
I clutch the rails of the fence, my gore dribs,
    thinn'd with the ooze of my skin,

I fall on the weeds and stones,
The riders spur their unwilling horses, haul close,
Taunt my dizzy ears and beat me violently over
the head with whip-stocks.

Old age superbly rising! O welcome, ineffable
grace of dying days!

See ever so far, there is limitless space outside of
that,
Count ever so much, there is limitless time around
that.
My rendezvous is appointed, it is certain,
The Lord will be there and wait till I come on
perfect terms.
The great Camerado, the lover true for whom I
pine will be there.

And whoever walks a furlong without sympathy
walks to his own funeral drest in his shroud.

And to glance with an eye or show a bean in its
pod confounds the learning of all times,
And there is no trade or employment but the
young man following it may become a hero,
And there is no object so soft but it makes a hub
for the wheel'd universe.
And I say to any man or woman, "Let your soul
stand cool and composed before a million
universes."

I see something of God each hour of the twenty-
four, and each moment then,

In the faces of men and women I see God, and in
my own face in the glass,
I find letters from God dropt in the street, and
every one is sign'd by God's name,
And I leave them where they are, for I know that
wheresoe'er I go,
Others will punctually come forever and ever.

Listener up there! What have you to confide
in me?
Look in my face while I snuff the sidle of evening.
(Talk honestly, no one else hears you, and I stay
only a minute longer.)
Who has done his day's work? Who will soonest
be through with his supper?
Who wishes to walk with me?

I too am not a bit tamed, I too am untrans-
latable,
I sound my barbaric yawp over the roofs of the
world.

INDEX